Xmas

Cake and Cookie

COOKBOOK

EASY AND TASTY HOLIDAYS AND CHRISTMAS COOKIES, CAKES, PIES, CANDIES, FUDGE,& MORE. AMAZE YOUR FAMILY AND CELEBRATE THE MOST WONDERFUL TIME OF THE YEAR WITH THEM.

Table of Contents

Introduction

Christmas, which falls on the 25th of December, is both a holy religious holiday and a cultural and commercial concept that is observed all over the world. More than two millennia of traditions and practices, both religious and secular, have been observed by people all over the world. The birth of Jesus of Nazareth, a religious leader whose teachings form the foundation of the Christian faith, is marked on Christmas Day by Christians.

Christmas traditions include swapping gifts, decorating trees, going to church, eating with loved ones, and, of course, having to wait for Santa Claus to show up. Since 1870, the 25th of December has been observed to celebrate the birth of Jesus Christ as a federal holiday in the United States.
So experimenting with different recipes for Christmas Eve cakes and cookies can be a lot of fun. This cookbook contains many different holiday meals that you should try.

Recipes

Here are some delicious cakes and cookies recipes which you can make and enjoy on Christmas:

1. Bûche de Noël (Yule Log Cake)

Preparation Time:

40 mins

Total Time:

3 hrs

Servings:

Eight Svcs

Ingredients:

FOR THE CAKE
- Powdered sugar for sprinkling
- Cooking spray
- six big eggs, separated
- 1/4 teaspoon cup of granulated sugar split
- half a cup of all-purpose flour
- a quarter teaspoon of kosher salt; and dusting sugar.

FOR THE FILLING
- One-quarter cups of sour cream
- One-fourth cup of icing sugar
- Optional gelatin, 2 tablespoons
- One teaspoon of real vanilla extract and a dash of kosher salt

FOR THE FROSTING AND DECORATING
- ½ cup of melted butter in one stick
- Additional powdered sugar (up to 1 1/2 cups) for garnish
- 5 tablespoons chocolate powder.
- One teaspoon of vanilla extract
- 3 tablespoons heavy cream
- A dash of kosher salt
- Chocolate curls as an ornament
- As a garnish, cranberries
- Miniature rosemary sprigs for decoration

Directions:

- Turn the oven's temperature up to 350 degrees. A jelly roll pan should be lined with parchment paper and cooking spray before being left to cool. Salt, cocoa powder, and flour should all be combined in a medium bowl.
- Egg yolks should be fluffyly beaten in a big bowl in order to thicken them. Beat till pale after gradually incorporating 12 cups of sugarfollowed by the flour mixture, which is then beaten until smooth. In a different large bowl, beat the egg whites until soft peaks form. When you reach stiff peaks, gently add the

remaining Fourteen sugar cups. Two distinct batches of egg whites should be folded into the batter, each one at a time.

- Spread the batter evenly in the pan after you've finished preparing it. Bake for 12 minutes till the top springs around when lightly tapped.

- Sift confectioners' sugar over a fresh kitchen towel, then flip the heated cake onto it. The baking sheet's parchment paper should be removed.

- Use a towel to firmly roll the cake into a log, beginning at the short end. Let it cool down completely before continuing.

- In a shallow microwave-safe ball, combine 2 tablespoons of cold water with 2 tablespoons of gelatin to make the filling. Don't overheat the gelatin; instead, let it bloom for 5 to 10 minutes. Then, zap it in the microwave for 10 seconds to make it runny.

- In a large bowl, combine the heavy cream, sugar, pure vanilla extract, and a dash of salt. Beat these ingredients until they form medium peaks, then fold in the whipped cream. If gelatin is being used, drain it beforehand and stir it into the whipping cream while it continues to be whisked. Until you're ready to eat it, refrigerate.

- When the cake has cooled, unroll it and pour the filling evenly over it. Roll the cake back into a log with the aid of the towel. Place on a baking sheet in the refrigerator seam side down for one hour.

- In a big bowl, whip the butter until it is completely smooth to make the frosting. Add the sugar and cocoa powders, and stir until there are no lumps left. Next, beat until smooth and creamy while adding vanilla, heavy cream, and salt.

- Before serving, trim the cake's ends and cover it in chocolate buttercream. Finish with chocolate curls and a light dusting of powdered sugar. Put rosemary and cranberries on the log to make mistletoe.

2. Red Velvet Cake

Preparation Time:

10 mins

Total Time:

1 hrs 30 mins

Servings:

40 mins

Ingredients:

<u>**FOR THE CAKE**</u>
- Cooking sputter
- 1 cup (2 sticks) softened butter
- 1 c. granulated sugar
- 2 large eggs
- 1 cup of granulated sugar
- 2 large eggs
- One teaspoon of vanilla extract
- All-purpose flour, 2 cups
- Dutch-processed cocoa powder, 1/3 cup
- 1 tablespoon baking soda
- 1 tablespoon kosher salt
- One cup of buttermilk
- 1 tablespoon white vinegar, distilled
- Two tablespoons of red food dye

FOR CREAM CHEESE FROSTING

- 2 (8-ounce) blocks softened cream cheese
- 1/2 cup (1 stick) softened butter
- 4 cups powdered sugar
- 1 teaspoon pure vanilla essence
- 1/4 teaspoon kosher salt.

Directions:

- In a separate big basin, combine the flour, cocoa, and baking soda. Mix the wet ingredients with half of the dry ingredients until just mixed. Add the remaining dry ingredients.
- Buttermilk, vinegar, and red food colouring should be beaten in. Include the remaining dry goods.
- After 25 to 30 minutes of baking, depending on the size of the pans, simply insert a toothpick into the centre, and it should come out clean. Remove from heat and allow it cool entirely for 15 minutes on a cooling rack.

- In the meantime, make the frosting by using a hand mixer to blend the cream cheese and butter in a big bowl (or in the bowl of a stand mixer). Beat in powdered sugar to make icing that is airy and light. Salt and vanilla should be added, then combined thoroughly. If additional powdered sugar is required after the frosting has reached the proper thickness and spreadability, add it in 1/4 cup increments.
- Once the cakes have been sliced, flatten the tops with a serrated knife, keeping the scraps for decoration. Place the first layer of cake on a cake stand or serving platter and top with a thick layer of frosting. Both the top and the bottom of the cake should be frosted.The cake's sides can be adorned with a layer of crumbled cake.

3. Flourless Peanut Butter Chocolate Cake

Preparation Time:

10 mins

Total Time:

1 hrs 45 mins

Servings:

12 Svcs

Ingredients:

- Cooking sputter
- 6 ounces of roughly chopped bittersweet chocolate
- 1 stick of 1/2 c. butter
- 3 tablespoons of smooth peanut butter in addition to 1/2 cup
- 1 cup of sugar, granulated
- Four big eggs
- Half a cup of unsweetened chocolate powder, ideally Dutch-process
- chocolate chips, 3/4 cup
- Heavy cream, 6 tablespoons

Directions:

- Cooking spray can coat an 8-inch springform pan before placing it in the oven. Bring some water in a small pot to a boil over medium heat, then turn the heat down, and let the mixture simmer for a few minutes.
- On top of a simmering saucepan of water, lay a heatproof bowl containing chopped chocolate, peanut butter, and 12 cups of peanut butter. Stir the mixture until all of the chocolate has spread out and melted. Remove the pan from the heat source and take the bowl out of the pot.
- To avoid the mixture curdling, add the sugar and eggs one at a time, stirring vigorously after each addition. The cocoa powder should be added and thoroughly mixed in.
- When the batter is ready, pour it into the pan and spread it out evenly. Simply bake for the next 30 to 40 minutes. Take a break after that to allow it cool.
- Place the chocolate chips in a little heat-resistant bowl, and stir until melted. In a small saucepan over medium heat, combine chocolate and cream until the chocolate is smooth and melted. After letting it settle for a minute, whisk until smooth.
- Combine the remaining 3 tablespoons of peanut butter in a small microwave-safe bowl. Microwave for 15 seconds, stirring once halfway through.
- After taking the sides of the springform pan off, put the cake on a plate or tray. Distribute the ganache evenly over the cake using an offset spatula.

- Then use a small spoon, and spread peanut butter horizontally across the cake's ganache. Draw vertical striations in the ganache and peanut butter with a toothpick. Drag the mouse alternately from the top to the bottom and from the bottom to the top for each line. Allow it to sit for 15 minutes before slicing.

4. Peppermint Bark Cheesecake

Preparation Time:

40 mins

Total Time:

8 hrs

Servings:

12 svcs

Ingredients:

FOR THE CRUST
- 24 crushed Oreos
- 4 tablespoons melted butter
- a pinch of kosher salt

FOR THE CHEESECAKE
- Four softened 8-ounce blocks of cream cheese
- 3/4 cup of sugar, granulated
- Three big eggs
- 1/2 tablespoons peppermint extract
- 2 tablespoons of all-purpose flour
- 1/2 teaspoon of kosher salt
- Chunky, melting, and slightly chilly 9 oz. white chocolate
- 6 ounces of chopped semisweet chocolate
- A half-cup of chopped candy canes plus extra for the topping
- A whipped topping for decoration
- Choco shavings for decoration

Directions:

- Spray cooking oil liberally in an 8-inch baking dish, and preheat the oven to 325 degrees. In a big bowl, mix Oreos, butter, and salt. The bottom and sides of your prepared pan should be covered with the mixture you made in Step 1.
- Using a hand mixer or stand mixer with a paddle attachment, combine the cream cheese and sugar in a big basin and blend until smooth. Peppermint extract is added after the eggs have been added one time. Only mix the flour and salt after adding them. Add salt and flour.
- Once the white chocolate is smooth, add the semisweet chocolate and candy canes and fold until evenly distributed. Over the crust, pour the mixture.

- Place pan in a large braising pan and cover with aluminum foil. Add only enough boiling water to fill the baking pan halfway.

- Bake the cheesecake for approximately 1 hour and 20 minutes, or until the middle barely jiggles. After turning off the heat, put the cheesecake in the oven for an hour at room temperature.

- Remove the foil and refrigerate the cheesecake for at least five hours and up to overnight.

- After topping with cheesecake, glob extra whipped sprinkling around the edges.

- Add squashed candy canes and shavings of chocolate to the dessert before serving.

5. Flourless Chocolate Cake

Preparation Time:

10 mins

Total Time:

1 hrs 30 mins

Servings:

10 Svcs

Ingredients:

FOR THE CAKE
- Cooking sputter
- Roughly chopped six ounces of bittersweet chocolate
- 1/2 cup (1 stick) of butter, chunked up
- 1 teaspoon instant coffee powder
- 1/4 cup of hot water
- 1 cup of sugar, granulated
- Four big eggs
- Unsweetened cocoa powder, 3/4 cup (preferably Dutch process)

FOR THE GANACHE

- 1 cup of semisweet chocolate chips
- 1/2 cup of heavy cream
- Raspberries, used as a garnish

Directions:

- Grease an 8-inch springform pan with cooking spray, and preheat the oven to 350 degrees.
- Creating a cake: A small pot half-filled with water should be simmering on medium heat. A heat-resistant bowl should be placed over a pot of simmering water without the water touching the bottom of the bowl. In a medium saucepan over low heat, liquefy butter and chocolate while continually stirring. After removing the bowl from the pot, turn off the heat.
- Mix espresso powder into boiling water. Then mix the eggs into the melted chocolate by adding them and whisking. Add the cocoa powder and mix well.
- In the spring form pan that has been prepared, bake the batter for 35 minutes, or until the middle is set and a thin crust develops on top.
- Remove the cake from the springform pan, then allow it to cool for 15 minutes. Before slicing, let the cake cool fully.
- While waiting, make the ganache according to these instructions: In a small pan, heat heavy cream until it begins to simmer. In a heatproof bowl, pour hot cream over the chocolate chunks. Prior to combining, let the ingredients sit for one minute.
- Using a balanced spatula, spread the ganache over the cake.Refrigerate for 10 minutes, if desired, to set the sauce.
- To serve, sprinkle the raspberries on top.

6. Andes Chocolate Cake

Preparation Time:

10 mins

Total Time:

1 hrs 30 mins

Servings:

12 Svcs

Ingredients:

FOR THE CAKE
• 1 (16-oz) box of cake batter
• 1 cup of Andes mints + extras for decoration

FOR THE CHOCOLATE GANACHE
- 2 cups of chocolate chips
- 1 cup of heavy cream

FOR THE PEPPERMINT BUTTERCREAM
- Softened 1 cup of butter
- 5 cups of powdered sugar
- 1 teaspoon of peppermint extract
- 3 tablespoons of heavy cream
- 6 drops of green gel food colouring (optional)

Directions:

- Following the directions on the box, Make a chocolate cake with two 9-inch round layers.Allow for complete cooling.
- In a large saucepan, heat the heavy cream over medium heat until bubbles start to appear all over the rims. After pulling the dish off the heat and off the stove, whisk in the chocolate chunks. Allow the mixture to cool for at least 30 minutes to a spreadable consistency before icing the cake.
- Make Buttercream while you wait: To make the frosting, combine butter, powdered sugar, and Beat the peppermint extract in a big basin until it becomes frothy. Once the mixture is smooth, add the cream and green food colouring.
- Put buttercream icing on the first cake layer and the second one on the upper edge.
- Add a layer of ganache on top. You can leave the cake's sides bare or coat them in ganache, as demonstrated in the video.
- Andes mints are a perfect addition to your table cape.

7. Strawberry Cheesecake

Preparation Time:

15 mins

Total Time:

6 hrs 30 mins

Servings:

12 Svcs

Ingredients:

FOR THE CHEESECAKE
- 3 softened (8-oz) blocks of cream cheese
- 1 cup of sugar
- 3 big eggs
- 1/4 cup of sour cream
- 1 teaspoon of pure vanilla extract
- 1 teaspoon of lemon zest
- Sliced strawberries for garnish

FOR THE CRUST

- 15 crushed Graham Crackers
- 5 tablespoons melted butter
- 2 tablespoons granulated sugar
- a dash of kosher salt

FOR THE SAUCE
- 1 cup strawberry jam
- Water, 2 teaspoons (or lemon juice)

Directions:

- Grease a 9-inch spring form pan with cooking spray. Set the oven to 325 degrees.
- To make the cheesecake batter, use a hand mixer to thoroughly blend the cream cheese and sugar in a big basin. After beating the eggs, combine them with the sour cream, vanilla, and lemon zest.
- To prepare the crust, stir together the graham cracker crumbs, butter, sugar, and salt. Put cooking spray on the graham mixture before pressing it into a 9-inch springform pan. Over the crust, pour the cheesecake mixture.
- Bake for approximately 1 hour and 10 minutes, or until the middle jiggles. Remove the food from the oven after an hour and let it cool fully before putting it in the refrigerator for at least four hours or overnight.

- Stir in strawberry conserves and lemon juice to make a thick glaze. Till the mixture is silky and smooth, stir it continually.
- Prior to topping the cheesecake with strawberries, remove the glaze from them. Serve cold, sliced into wedges.

8. Chocolate Peanut butter Cheesecake

Preparation Time:

45 mins

Total Time:

7 hrs 25 mins

Servings:

10 to 12 svcs

Ingredients:

FOR THE CRUST
- 24 Oreos
- 3 tbsp. granulated sugar
- 1/8 teaspoon of kosher salt
- 5 tbsp. melted butter

FOR THE CHEESECAKE

- 4 (8-oz) packages of softened cream cheese
- 1 cup of packed light brown sugar
- 1/2 tsp. kosher salt
- 1 tablespoon of pure vanilla essence
- 4 large, room-temperature eggs
- One cup of creamy peanut butter
- 1/2 cup sour cream; 3/4 cup heavy cream
- Reese's Pieces for Garnish

FOR THE CHOCOLATE GANACHE
- 3/4 c. heavy cream
- 1/8 tsp. kosher salt
- 6 oz. finely chopped bittersweet or semisweet chocolate

Directions:

Making the Crust:

- The spring form pan's interior should be buttered. Oven: Position the center rack and heat to 350 degrees.
- Use a food processor or blender to grind Oreos into fine crumbs. Pulsing the mixture allows for the addition of salt and sugar. Blend with a fork or fingers until crumbs are evenly moistened in a medium bowl. Shove into the base and sides of the spring form pan about a third.
- Place the pan on a baking tray and bake the crust for ten min. While doing this, reduce the oven's heat to 325°F and place on a cooling rack.

- Boil some water in a small saucepan or tea kettle while you wait.

Making the Cheesecake:

- With a hand mixer or stand mixer equipped with the whisk attachment, beat the cream cheese for three to four minutes on medium, making an effort to scrape down the bowl as needed. Beat for 3 to 4 minutes, scraping down the bowl as necessary, after adding the sugar and salt. Add the vanilla extract at this point, and continue beating for a further 30 seconds.
- One at a time, beat the eggs, giving the bowl's bottom and sides a minute of scraping after each addition. Beat the peanut butter, sour cream, and heavy cream together with an electric mixer on low speed for a few minutes, or until the mixture is completely smooth and spotless. Before serving, take out of the fridge and use a spatula to smooth the top.
- Lay two sheets of aluminium foil over the springform pan before placing it in a sizable warming pan. Add enough boiling water to the springform pan to cover the sides halfway.
- For approximately 1 hour and 30 minutes, or until the top starts to brown and crack, bake the cheesecake. After shutting off the heat source, remove the cheesecake from the oven and allow it to cool for an hour in the water bath.
- The springform pan's foil should be removed before removing the roasting pan from the oven. Before serving, let the cheesecake warm up to room temperature.Cheesecake should be chilled for at least four hours, preferably overnight, after it cools to room temperature.

Assembling and Decorating of the Cheesecake:

- Edges of the springform pan should be removed, then placed aside until serving time. All that is required to add the chocolate is a medium bowl that is clean and dry.Warm the cream to a barely simmering temperature in a small saucepan over medium heat. Ten minutes after pouring warm cream over chocolate, add salt and mix until smooth.
- Allow some of the ganache to flow down the sides as you evenly distribute it over the cheesecake. Reese's Pieces can be added after.

9. Citrus upside-down Cake

Preparation Time:

20 mins

Total Time:

1 hrs 30 mins

Servings:

8 to 10 Svcs

Ingredients:

FOR FRUIT TOPPING
- Cooking spray
- 4-5 citrus fruits, such as a variety of oranges, grapefruits, or lemons
- 1/2 c. granulated sugar
- 4 tbsp. butter, melted

FOR CAKE BATTER
- All-purpose flour, 1 1/2 cups
- 1 teaspoon baking soda
- 1/2 teaspoon of kosher salt
- 1/2 cup (1 stick) softened butter
- 1/2 cup of sugar, granulated
- 1/4 cup of brown sugar in a bag
- Freshly chopped thyme, 1 1/2 tbsp
- zest from one orange
- Two big eggs
- One tablespoon of vanilla extract
- 3/4 a cup of buttermilk

Directions:

- The oven should be heated at 350 degrees Fahrenheit before anything else. Using parchment paper and oil, line a 9" round cake pan.Slice fruit about 1/8" thick. As many pith as possible should be cut off with a paring knife.
- A small bowl of sugar and melted butter is all that is needed for this recipe. Distribute the batter evenly across the base of your prepared pan using a spatula. Make a rosette of fruit on top and slightly overlap it, so the base is completely covered.
- In a larger basin, combine salt, baking powder, and flour.
- Using a hand mixer, beat the butter, sugars, thyme, and orange zest in a big bowl until frothy and light. After each addition of an egg, keep on beating. When the mixture is smooth, add the vanilla and whisk again.

- The batter should be almost fully incorporated before adding dry ingredients. Toss in buttermilk and beat to a smooth consistency, careful not to overwork the batter. Apply a thin coating of the batter to the fruit using a spatula.

- A wooden skewer inserted in the centre should come out clean after 35 to 40 minutes of baking. Flip onto a serving dish and allow cooling for 10 to 15 minutes. Allow for complete cooling.

10. Carrot Cake

Preparation Time:

10 mins

Total Time:

1 hrs 30 mins

Servings:

12 Svcs

Ingredients:

FOR THE CAKE
- Cooking sputter
- All-purpose flour, 3 cups
- 1.5 teaspoons kosher salt
- 2 teaspoons baking soda
- 2 teaspoons cinnamon
- Granulated sugar, 2 cups
- 1.5 cups of vegetable oil
- Four big eggs
- One teaspoon of vanilla extract
- Grated carrots, 3 cups
- 1 cup of pecans, roughly chopped, plus extras for decoration
- One cup raisins

FOR THE CREAM CHEESE FROSTING
- One (8-ounce) block of softened cream cheese
- 1/2 cup (1 stick) softened butter
- Pure vanilla extract (1 teaspoon)
- powdered sugar (4 cups)

Directions:

- Use cooking spray to prepare two 8-inch round cake pans, and bake at 350 degrees for 20 to 25 minutes. In a big bowl, combine the flour, salt, baking soda, and cinnamon.
- Using a hand mixer or a stand mixer, combine the sugar and oil in a separate large basin and beat until well combined.For each egg, beat it well before adding the next one, then stir in the vanilla. Dry ingredients should only be combined to the point of barely visible streaks of color. Fetch all elements jointly in a large bowl.
- Spread the batter evenly among the ready baking dishes using a spatula. After removing it from the oven, give it 45 minutes to cool. Before turning cakes upside down onto a cooling rack to continue cooling, give them 15 minutes to cool.

- In a big bowl, combine the cream cheese and butter and beat them with a hand mixer until they are frothy and light. The vanilla and icing sugar should be well combined before becoming spreadable.
- After the cake has been properly frosted, pecans can be used to garnish it.

11.Chocolate covered Cake Balls

Preparation Time:

45 mins

Total Time:

2 hrs 45 mins

Servings:

4 dozen

Ingredients:

- Cooking sputter
- One box of cake mixes plus the materials listed on the box
- 3/4 cup (one and a half sticks) softened vegan butter
- Powdered sugar, 3 cups
- 3 tablespoons vegan cream
- One teaspoon of vanilla extract
- A dash of kosher salt
- White chocolate chips, 2 cups
- Semisweet chocolate chips, 2 cups
- Divided 4 tablespoons coconut oil
- Decoration-related sprinkling

Directions:

- Place baking pan with cooking drizzle in a 9 by 13-inch baking dish, and then heat the oven to 350 degrees. The cake mix needs to be prepared as directed on the box, then distributed equally in a pan. Bake for 30 minutes, or until the centre of a toothpick inserted comes out clean. Slice only after complete cooling.
- Using a hand mixer, thoroughly combine the butter and sugar in a large basin. Combine all of the remaining ingredients, including the cream, vanilla, and salt. Add extra cream if the frosting is too thick.)
- A big baking sheet should be covered with parchment paper.To make the balls, combine the cake crumbs and frosting and form tablespoon-sized balls. Cool completely before serving on a parchment-lined baking sheet.

- In a big heatproof bowl, microwave white chocolate and 2 tablespoons coconut oil at 30 second intervals.Use semisweet chocolate in place of the bittersweet.

- Shake off any excess chocolate from the chilled cake balls before coating them in melted chocolate. Return to a baking sheet and decorate with sprinkles right away. Chill for about 15 minutes to arrange the ice cubes.

12.   Healthy Chocolate Cake

Preparation Time:

15 mins

Total Time:

1 hrs 30 mins

Servings:

12 Svcs

Ingredients:

FOR THE CAKE
spray for frying
1/2 a cup of almond flour
2/3 c. unsweetened cocoa powder
Coconut flour, 3/4 cup
Flaxseed meal, 1/4 cup
Baking powder, 2 teaspoons
Baking soda, 2 teaspoons
kosher salt, 1 teaspoon
Softened 1/2 cup (1 stick) of vegan butter
4 large eggs and 3/4 cup keto-friendly granulated sugar
Pure vanilla extract, 1 teaspoon
Almond milk, 1 cup
strong coffee, 1/3 cup
FOR THE BUTTERCREAM
2 (8-oz) blocks of softened cream cheese
Softened 1/2 cup (1 stick) of butter
Keto-friendly 3/4 cup of powdered sugar
Unsweetened cocoa powder in a half-cup
Coconut flour, 1/4 cup
Instant coffee powder, 1/4 teaspoon
heavy cream, 3/4 cup
Kosher salt, a pinch

Directions:

- Line two 8-inch baking pans with parchment paper and coat them with cooking spray prior to baking. In a sizable mixing bowl, combine all the ingredients and stir well to combine them all.
- To make butter and sugar frothy and light, combine them in a second big bowl and whisk with a hand-held mixer. Utilizing the vanilla essence as a guide, add each egg separately. After adding the dry ingredients, stir in the milk and coffee.

- Depending on the size of your pans, bake for 28 minutes or until a toothpick inserted in the centre comes out clean. Before continuing, let it warm up to room temperature.

How to make the icing:

- Using a hand mixer, combine the butter and cream cheese in a large bowl until they are perfectly smooth. It is crucial to thoroughly combine all the components until no lumps remain. Cream and a pinch of salt should be added and thoroughly mixed up.

- Top the cake layer with a thick layer of buttercream by spreading it on with a big knife. After adding a second layer, ice the cake's sides.

- Store the food in the refrigerator until you're ready to serve it for the best results.

13. Candy Cane Cheesecake

Preparation Time:

30 mins

Total Time:

8 hrs

Servings:

8 to 10 Svcs

Ingredients:

FOR THE CHEESECAKE
- 3 softened 8-ounce bars of cream cheese
- 1 cup of sugar
- Three big eggs
- 1/4 cup of sour cream
- 1 teaspoon peppermint oil
- 2 tablespoons of all-purpose flour
- 1 tablespoon kosher salt
• Half a cup of crushed candy canes

FOR THE CRUST
- 1 sleeve of crumbled Graham crackers
- Melted butter, 5 tablespoons
- 1/4 cup of sugar
- kosher salt pinch

FORT THE TOPPING
• Whipped cream for drizzling
• Candy canes in crushed form for garnish

Directions:

- Spray cooking spray in an 8" or 9" baking pan before putting it in the oven at 325ºF. The pan is set on a baking sheet and has its bottom covered in aluminium foil. The cheesecake filling is made by: Using a hand mixer or a stand mixer with a paddle attachment, combine cream cheese and sugar in a big basin. Add the eggs one at a time, then the flour and peppermint extract. Use a fork to stir in the crushed candy canes.
- The crust is prepared. In a sizable basin, thoroughly combine the graham cracker crumbs, melted butter, sugar, and salt. In the pan you just prepared, pour the batter and press it down firmly.

• After distributing the filling over the crust, wait a few minutes before serving. The cheesecake should barely jiggle when touched in the centre after baking for 1 hour and 30 minutes. As an alternative, you might bake the cheesecake in a deep baking dish. Fill the baking pan with hot water until it is halfway full. Remove the aluminium foil from the cheesecake once it has cooled in the oven for an hour. Refrigerate the cheesecake in the pan for at least 5 hours and ideally overnight to allow it to set.

- Crushed candy canes and whipped cream can be used to decorate the cheesecake.

14.   Icebox Cake

Preparation Time:

5 mins

Total Time:

4 hrs 20 mins

Servings:

8 Svcs

Ingredients:

- 3 cups of chilled heavy cream
- 1 teaspoon pure vanilla extract
- One teaspoon of vanilla extract
- 64 chocolate or Oreo wafers

Directions:

- Using a hand mixer, combine heavy whipping cream, powdered sugar, and vanilla extract to form stiff peaks (or stand mixer fitted with a whisk attachment).
- A thin layer of whipped cream should be placed on the bottom of an 8-inch springform pan.followed by an even thin coat of whole Oreos or cookies. For this recipe, you'll need four layers of cookies, so disperse more whipped cream on top.
- Whip up a final layer of cream and spread it over the cake. Chill the cake for about 4 hours.

- To serve, top with squashed cookies and cut into squares.

15.   Reese's Explosion Cake

Preparation Time:

30 mins

Total Time:

1 hrs 5 mins

Servings:

10 to 12 Svcs

Ingredients:

FOR THE CAKE
- Pan cooking spray
- One box of Devil's Food Cake
- one container of chocolate pudding
- one cup of sour cream, four big eggs
- half a cup of water
- ten Reese's Peanut Butter Cups cut in half
- half a cup of Reese's Pieces for topping

FOR THE PEANUT BUTTER FROSTING
- Unsalted butter, two cups
- Powdered sugar, 8 cups
- One quarter cup of creamy peanut butter
- 7 tablespoons whole milk
• kosher salt pinch

FOR THE GANACHE
- 3/4 cup of thick cream
- Semisweet chocolate chips: 1 1/2 cups

Directions:

- Spray cooking spray into two 9-inch cake pans and preheat the oven to 350 degrees. In a big bowl, whisk together the eggs, water, and cake mix. The combination must be well-rounded.
- Bake the cake for 33 to 35 minutes, or until a toothpick inserted in the middle comes out clean. Go to a wire rack to finish cooling.
- Making the icing is as follows: A hand mixer is used to cream the butter in a separate sizable bowl. Half of the powdered sugar is added and well blended after the mixture has been smoothed out. Add half of the milk and the peanut butter, then mix well. Salt and extra powdered sugar should be beaten in. (If required, add more milk to the frosting to thin it down.

- Next, heat the heavy cream in a small saucepan over low heat until it bubbles. In a tiny heatproof bowl, pour hot, heavy cream on top of the chocolate chunks. After 2 minutes, whip until the mixture is smooth and clump-free.

- To assemble the cake, level the cake layers using a sizable serrated knife. To finish assembling the cake, spread some frosting on a cardboard cake circle and top it with the first layer of cake.

- Top the cake with a uniform layer of 1 cup frosting. After the second cake layer is on top, cover the outside of the cake with the leftover frosting.

- Use ganache to swirl and smooth the cake's top before drizzling it down the sides. You'll need this line of frosting to build around to make the candy rings.

- Put some of your favorite candy on top of the frosting.

16.   Black Forest Cake

Preparation Time:

30 mins

Total Time:

2 hrs 30 mins

Servings:

16 Svcs

Ingredients:

FOR THE CAKE + SYRUP
two boxes of food cake mix plus the additional ingredients listed on the box
One 24-ounce jar of tart cherries
Granulated sugar, half a cup
1/4 cup of kirsch

FOR THE FROSTING + TOPPING
- 3 teaspoons of plain gelatin
- Heavy whipping cream, 4 cups
- Powdered sugar, 1 cup
- One teaspoon of vanilla extract
- Fresh cherries for topping
- Chocolate shavings for topping

Directions:

How to prepare a cake:

- Turn the oven's dial to 350 degrees Fahrenheit. To prevent sticking, line three 9-inch round cake pans with parchment paper and coat them with cooking spray.
- Cake mixes should be prepared according to the directions on the package. Bake as directed on the package or until a wooden skewer inserted into the centre of the cake comes out clean. Cakes should be turned over onto wire racks to continue cooling ten minutes after being taken out of the oven.

While you wait, you can start making syrup:

- Remove all but 1/2 cup of juice from the cherries using a strainer and discard the rest. Save the cherries for the cake assembly. 12 cups of sugar should be put in a small saucepan and heated to a boil. To dissolve the sugar, stir it into the hot water. After adding the kirsch, turn the heat off.
How to make the icing:

- In a medium heatproof bowl, combine 1/4 cup boiling water with the gelatin to dissolve it. Microwave the gelatin for increments of 5 seconds to completely dissolve it. The heavy cream and powdered sugar must be well mixed in order to form soft peaks. Put a little vanilla in the mixture. When the cream has reached stiff peaks, slowly fold in the gelatin mixture and continue beating until everything is thoroughly incorporated.
- Make a pastry bag with a star tip and place 1 cup of frosting.
- Brush the cherry syrup liberally over the top of one layer of cake before serving. Put 1 1/4 cups of frosting on top of the cake.Using the rest of the cherries, cover the dish. Repeat with a second cake layer on top. Before dusting the remaining cake layer with powdered sugar, brush a thick coating of syrup over the cake's top. Sprinkle the leftover icing over the top and sides to complete the cake.
- Before sprinkling it on top, press the shaved chocolate into the sides of the cake.

• Using the remaining frosting, pipe dollops of icing all the way around the cake's top. Place a fresh cherry on top of each dollop.

17.   S'mores Cake

Preparation Time:

30 mins

Total Time:

1 hrs 30 mins

Servings:

12 Svcs

Ingredients:

FOR THE CAKE
- Pan cooking spray
- 1 1/4 cups softened butter
- 1 cup of loosely jarred brown sugar
- 1 cup of sugar, granulated
- Four big eggs
- Two teaspoons of vanilla extract
- All-purpose flour, 2 cups
- Graham cracker crumbs, 1 cup
- 2 tablespoons baking powder
- 1 tablespoon kosher salt
- One cup of buttermilk

FOR THE FROSTING + DECORATION
- 1 1/2 cups of softened butter
- Unsweetened cocoa powder, 1 cup
- Two teaspoons of vanilla extract
- A dash of kosher salt
- 3.75 cups of powdered sugar
- 1/3 cup to 1/2 cup of heavy cream
- 3 cups of marshmallow cream
- Graham cracker crumbs, 1/4 cup

Directions:

Making a cake:

- Turn the oven's dial to 350 degrees Fahrenheit. Three 8-inch cake pans should be greased and lined with parchment paper. In a big bowl, whisk the butter and sugars using a hand or stand mixer until they are light and fluffy. After each addition, make careful to fully beat the eggs. Blend in the vanilla essence completely.

- In a different big basin, mix the flour, graham cracker crumbs, baking soda, and salt. Mix the wet ingredients with half of the dry ingredients until the batter is just combined. One the buttermilk is added, whip the mixture once more to ensure complete blending. Mix in the remaining dry ingredients at a low speed.

• Divide the batter among the pans and bake for 30 minutes, or until the tops are golden and a wooden skewer inserted in the centre comes out clean, whichever comes first. After that, flip each cake onto a cooling rack and let it finish cooling.

How to make the icing:

- Using a hand mixer, combine butter, cocoa powder, vanilla, and salt in a sizable bowl. As you gradually add it, beat in the powdered sugar until completely blended. (Its texture will be crumbly!)The frosting should be smooth before adding the heavy cream in stages.

Assembling the cake:

- On your cake plate or serving platter, place the first layer of cake on top of a dollop of frosting. Apply a thin layer of frosting to the cake.To make it easier to spread, microwave marshmallow creme for 20 seconds. To prevent marshmallow crème from oozing out, spread a thin layer of marshmallow crème over frosting, leaving a 1/2" border all around. To finish the cake, repeat the layering process. Frost the entire cake and then top it with marshmallow crème, spreading it to the cake's edges.
- Using a kitchen torch, toast the cake's drips and sprinkle graham cracker crumbs on the cake's top.

18. Ugly Sweater Cake

Preparation Time:

30 mins

Total Time:

1 hrs 10 mins

Servings:

8 Svcs

Ingredients:

- Pan cooking spray
- 1 box of chocolate cake mix plus the additional ingredients listed on the box
- 3 cups vanilla buttercream
- 6 drops of food colouring in red
- To decorate, use Hershey Kisses
- M&Ms, for use in decoration
- To decorate, use candy stars
- Decoration-related sprinkling
- Teddy Grahams, for use as décor
- Rolos as a decorative item
- Small marshmallows for decorating

Directions:

- Turn the oven's dial to 350 degrees Fahrenheit. A 9-by-13-inch pan should be lined with parchment paper, then greased and sprayed with cooking spray. Bake the chocolate cake batter in the pan in accordance with the directions on the package.
- Bake the cake for roughly 20 to 25 minutes, or until a wooden skewer inserted into it comes out clean.Permit it to cool down to room temperature before proceeding on.
- Approximately 2 cups of vanilla frosting were blended with red food colouring in a medium bowl. The remaining 1 cup of vanilla frosting should be piped using a piping bag and a large star attachment.
- Scattered the red frosting evenly and smoothly over the cooled cake with an offset spatula. Vanilla frosting with a white tip creates the sweater's neckline and middle.

- After creating the buttons with Hershey's Kisses, decorate the sweater on the left and right sides with M&Ms, candy stars, sprinkles, Teddy Grahams, Rolos, and mini marshmallows.Recreate around with it and arrive up with something extraordinary!
- Serve at room temperature, sliced into rectangles.

19.   S'mores Mousse Cake

Preparation Time:

10 mins

Total Time:

4 hrs 45 mins

Servings:

10 Svcs

Ingredients:

FOR THE CRUST
- 1 sleeve of Graham crackers, around 1 1/2 cups, finely crushed
- 1/4 c. granulated sugar
- 5 tbsp. melted butter

FOR THE CHOCOLATE MOUSSE
- 2 teaspoons of plain gelatin
- 2.5 tablespoons cold water
- 2.5 cups of chocolate chips
- Divided 3 cups of heavy cream
- 0.5 cups of powdered sugar
- FOR THE MERINGUE
- 3 substantial egg whites
- 1/4 cup of sugar, granulated
- 1/4 teaspoon of cream of tartar

Directions:

Making the Crust:

- Grains of salt and sugar are mixed with butter until the consistency of coarse sand is in a medium-sized bowl. Spread the ingredients evenly in a springform pan that measures 8 or 9 inches.
- To make a chocolate mousse: In a small basin, mix the gelatin and water; let it stand for five to ten minutes.
- Meanwhile, in a heatproof bowl, combine the chocolate chips. A small saucepan over medium-high heat should be used to bring 1 cup of heavy cream to a simmer before turning off the heat.Softened gelatin should be whisked into the mixture until it is completely dissolved. Pour the liquid over the melted chocolate chips, then whisk the mixture again until it is smooth. As the mixture cools, stir it occasionally.
- Using a stand mixer with a stirring attachment or a large mixing bowl and a hand mixer, whip 2 cups of cream and powdered sugar until firm peaks form. The melted chocolate mixture should be combined with 1/4 cup of whipped cream. Remaining whipped cream should be added and properly mixed.Put aside in the refrigerator for at least four hours.

Making a meringue:

- Combine the egg whites, sugar, and cream of tartar in a heat-resistant bowl. Place the bowl over a small saucepan of simmering water to make a double boiler, being careful to keep the bowl's bottom away from the water.Whisk till the sugar is completely dissolved and the mixture reaches 160°F. Remove from the oven.

- For roughly three minutes, whip the egg whites and sugar until stiff peaks form.

- Take out the cake and top with the meringue. To toast meringue, use a kitchen torch.

20.   Tres Leches Cake

Preparation Time:

15 mins

Total Time:

2 hrs 45 mins

Servings:

12 Svcs

Ingredients:

FOR THE CAKE
- Cooking sputter
- All-purpose flour, 1 1/2 cups
- 1.5 teaspoons of baking powder
- 1/2 teaspoon of kosher salt
- Five big eggs, divided
- 1 1/4 cups of split granulated sugar
- One teaspoon of vanilla extract
- ½ cup milk
• 4 tablespoons of melted, chilled butter

FOR THE FILLING
- 1 can of sweetened condensed milk, 14 ounces
- One 12-ounce can of evaporated milk
- 1/2 cup milk
- One teaspoon of vanilla extract

FOR THE WHIPPED CREAM
- 2 cups of heavy cream
- 1/2 cup of sugar, granulated

FOR SERVING
• 1/4 c. sugar and cinnamon
• strawberry slices for serving

Directions:

Making the cake:
- Pour cooking drizzle onto a 9" x 13" baking pan and preheat the oven to 350º. In a big basin, combine salt, baking powder, and flour.
- Using a hand mixer, beat the egg yolks and 1 cup of sugar in a separate large bowl until stiff ribbons form behind the beaters. Add the vanilla extract and set the bowl aside.
• In a third large bowl, whip the egg whites until soft peaks form. Add the remaining 1/4 cup sugar and whisk until stiff peaks form.

- The dry components should be combined with the egg yolk mixture. Milk and melted butter are added; beat until smooth. Don't overwork the egg whites, please. A wooden skewer inserted in the centre of the cake should come out clean after 30 minutes of baking.
- Allow time for cooling to occur.

While you're waiting, prepare the filling:

• Combine milk, evaporated milk, sweetened condensed milk, and vanilla in a medium basin and whisk to combine. After making fork holes all over the cake, evenly pour the milk mixture over it. For at least an hour, let the mixture sit in the covered refrigerator.

- Prepare a batch of whipped cream to be served: With a hand mixer, combine heavy cream and sugar in a big bowl and beat until stiff peaks form.Sprinkle cinnamon sugar over the whipped cream frosting. Serve with fresh fruit, such as strawberries.

21.   Chocolate Peppermint Cheesecake

Preparation Time:

30 mins

Total Time:

7 hrs

Servings:

8 to 10 Svcs

Ingredients:

- Cooking spray
- 3 (8-ounce) blocks of softened cream cheese
- 1 cup of sugar, granulated
- 2 big eggs
- 1/4 cup sour cream
- 1 1/2 tbsp all-purpose flour
- 1/4 tsp kosher salt
- 1 tsp peppermint essence
- 1/2 cup chopped chocolate, with additional for decoration.
- 1/2 cup of white chocolate, with additional pieces for garnish
- A half-cup of chopped candy canes plus extras for decoration

FOR THE OREO CRUST
- 24 Oreo peppermints
- Melted butter, 5 tablespoons

FOR THE CHOCOLATE GANACHE
- 3/4 cup of heated heavy cream
- Semisweet chocolate chips: 1 1/2 cups

Directions:

- Spray an 8-inch pan with cooking spray, then preheat the oven to 350ºF. Close the gaps: With a hand mixer, combine cream cheese and sugar in a large bowl (or stand mixer fitted with a paddle attachment). Beat each egg in turn with an electric mixer before incorporating the sour cream, flour, vanilla, and peppermint essence. Add the candy canes and chocolate chips, then set the mixture aside to chill.
- To make a crust, adhere to these instructions: The Oreos can be placed in a large Ziploc bag or processed in a food processor to create fine crumbs.Incorporate the butter into the batter and mix thoroughly.
- Pack the crust firmly into the pan after it has been prepared.

- After that, place the pan on a baking sheet with a rim and bake for an additional 20 minutes at 350ºF. Bake for approximately an hour, or until the middle is just wobbly. Place the springform pan in a roasting pan with a deep bottom after wrapping it in aluminium foil. Place the springform pan in the roasting pan, fill it halfway with boiling water, and then put it in the oven to bake.

•After an hour of baking, take the cheesecake out of the oven.
•To make sure the cheesecake is thoroughly set, chill it in the refrigerator for at least 4 hours and ideally all night.

- To serve with the dish, make a chocolate ganache. Pour the heated cream over the chocolate chips and stir until all the chocolate has melted, about 5 minutes.Refrigerate 5 minutes if the ganache is too thin.)

- Sprinkle with more minced chocolate and candy canes and disperse ganache over chilled cheesecake.

- Refrigerate the ganache for 10 minutes before serving to set.

22. Delicious Fruitcake

Preparation Time:

15 mins

Total Time:

2 hrs

Servings:

6 to 8 Svcs

Ingredients:

CAKE
- 1/2 cup chopped pecans
    - 1/2 cup chopped pistachios
    - 1/2 cup chopped slivered almonds
    - 1/2 cup (1 stick) softened butter
    - 1/2 cup packed light brown sugar
    - 1/2 cup granulated sugar
    - 3 large eggs
    - 2 teaspoons pure vanilla extract
    - 2 cups all-purpose flour
    - 1 teaspoon baking powder
    - 1/2 teaspoon Kosher salt
    - 1/4 teaspoon cinnamon
    - 1/4 teaspoon nutmeg
    - 2 tablespoons bourbon
    - 1/2 cup chopped dried cranberries
    - 1/2 cup chopped

POWDERED SUGAR GLAZE
- Powdered sugar: 1 1/4 cups
- heavy cream: 3 tablespoons

Directions:

- Set the oven rack in the middle and preheat the oven to 350 degrees Fahrenheit to begin preparing it. A sizable baking sheet should be filled with almonds and pistachios. Golden brown after 10 to 12 minutes of toasting. Remain calm.

- Lower the oven's setting to 300 degrees Fahrenheit. Cooking spray should be applied to the pan before using it for this recipe. In a big basin, whisk the butter and sugars together. Incorporate the eggs and vanilla completely into the mixture by beating them in. Separately combine the flour, baking powder, salt, and spices.

- After the dry ingredients have been incorporated in, whisk in the bourbon. Toasted fruit and nuts provide a delightful touch to this recipe. Approximately 45 to an hour of baking time results in a toothpick put into the cake coming out clean. Ten minutes of cooling time must pass before inverting onto a cooling rack to complete cooling.
- In a bowl, combine powdered sugar and heavy cream. Whisk until combined. Add a small amount of heavy cream until the desired consistency is achieved. Glaze the cake after it has been allowed to cool.

23.   Hot Cocoa Poke Cake

Preparation Time:

15 mins

Total Time:

45 mins

Servings:

2 to 3 Svcs

Ingredients:

1 box of chocolate cake mix plus the other ingredients listed on the box
Two cups of marshmallow creme
Heavy cream and one tablespoon of water
Hot cocoa mix in two packets
14 cup of marshmallow pieces
Choco shavings, two tablespoons

Directions:

- Turn the oven on to 350 degrees and oil a 9 by 13-inch baking pan. To prepare chocolate cake mix, follow the directions on the package. Bake for 25 minutes, or until a wooden skewer inserted in the centre comes out clean.
- Pierce the cake with the bottom of a spoon to create holes all over it.Microwave the marshmallow creme and water for 10 seconds in a small bowl, then stir to combine thoroughly. Assure that all of the gaps in the cake have been filled before spreading the glaze over the top.
- Combine your ingredients in a sizable basin, including the heavy cream, salt, and chocolate powder. Surpassed till the soft peaks form, 3 to 4 minutes with a hand mixer. Garnish with marshmallow and chocolate shavings, and whipped cream before serving. Serve.

24.　Champagne Cake

Preparation Time:

15 mins

Total Time:

2 hrs 15 mins

Servings:

12 servings

Ingredients:

FOR CAKE
- Cooking sputter
- All-purpose flour, 1 1/4 cups
- 1/four cup cornstarch
- 2 tablespoons baking powder
- 1/2 teaspoon of kosher salt
- Three substantial egg whites, at room temperature
- 2/3 cup room temperature Champagne or Prosecco
- One teaspoon of vanilla extract
- granulated sugar, 1 1/3 cup
- 1 1/2 sticks of softened 3/4 cup butter
- 1 tablespoon lemon zest
- sugar sanding as a garnish

FOR FROSTING
- Powdered sugar, 5 cups
- 1 1/2 cups (3 sticks) softened butter
- 1/4 cup of sour cream
- One teaspoon of vanilla extract
- One cup of cut strawberries
- A pinch of kosher salt

Directions:

- Set the oven to 350ºF before beginning to prepare it. Cooking spray two 8-inch cake pans before lining them with parchment paper.

- Create a confection: In a larger basin, combine the flour, cornstarch, baking powder, and salt. In a another medium dish, whisk the egg whites and champagne simultaneously.
- Using a hand mixer, combine sugar and butter in a sizable basin until light and silky, 2 to 3 minutes. It is best to add the flour mixture first, then the egg mixture, and so on. The batter should be divided amongst

the prepared cake pans before the lemon zest is added. Cakes should be baked for 30 minutes, or until they loosen from the pans. Place on a cooling rack and shift out after 30 minutes to finish cooling.

- Using a hand mixer, blend the powdered sugar, butter, sour cream, vanilla, and salt in a sizable basin. 1 cup frosting and 1 cup of chopped strawberries should be combined in a medium bowl; set aside.
- Spread strawberry frosting on the bottom cake layer before adding the top one. Frost the cake's top and sides; save any leftover frosting for the top in a piping bag with a star tip.The outside of the cake should be covered in a thick layer of frosting. Serve with clear sanding sugar if desired.

25. Red Velvet Cookie Cake

Preparation Time:

20 mins

Total Time:

1 hrs 10 mins

Servings:

10 to 12 servings

Ingredients:

FOR THE COOKIE CAKE
- 3/4 cup softened salted butter
- 1 cup of sugar
- 1 big egg
- 1 teaspoon vanilla bean extract
- 2 teaspoons vinegar
- 1 1/2 tablespoons of red food dye
- Two and a quarter cups of all-purpose flour
- 2 teaspoons cornstarch
- 1 teaspoon baking soda
- 1 tablespoon cacao powder
- 1/4 teaspoon of kosher salt
- 3 tablespoons sprinkles, plus extra for decoration

FOR THE CREAM CHEESE FROSTING
- 4 ounces softened cream cheese
- 3 tablespoons softened butter
- 2 cups powdered sugar
- Half a teaspoon of pure vanilla extract

Directions:

• Use parchment paper to line a 9-inch cake pan, and preheat the oven to 350 degrees. It's time to grease every joint.

• In a large bowl, beat the butter and sugar with a hand mixer until light and fluffy, about 3 to 4 minutes. Mix the egg, vanilla, vinegar, salt, and red food colouring in a thorough manner. Now combine flour, cocoa powder, and baking soda in a medium bowl and whisk to combine. Next, add the dry ingredients to the wet ones and stir to combine.

- Cookie dough should be refrigerated for 30 minutes to an hour before adding sprinkles. Cake pans should be pressed evenly with dough.
- The edges will be hard after 18 to 20 minutes.
- Before moving the cake to a serving dish, allow it to cool completely in the pan.
- Beat the cream cheese and butter together until they form a smooth frosting. Using an electric mixer, gradually add half the powdered sugar and blend until smooth. Add the remaining powdered sugar and vanilla extract and blend again until well blended.
- Serve with additional sprinkles on the cookie cake's edges. Chill until prepared to serve in an airtight container.

26.   Cannoli Cake

Preparation Time:

1 hrs

Total Time:

1 hrs 45 mins

Servings:

12 servings

Ingredients:

CAKE
- Unsalted butter, 3/4 cup
- All-purpose flour
- kosher salt
- 1 tablespoon baking powder are required
- 1 1/2 cups of sugar, granulated
- Six big eggs
- Almond Extract, 1 teaspoon
- 1.25 cups of half-and-half
- 1 cup of miniature chocolate chips
- 1 cup of miniature chocolate chips
- 2 substantial cannoli shells

FROSTING
- Whole-milk ricotta, 3 1/2 cups
- 2.5 teaspoons orange zest
- Lemon zest, 2 teaspoons
- 1/4 teaspoon cinnamon
- 1/4 teaspoon of kosher salt
- 3/4 cups of confectioners' sugar
- 3/4 cup of thick cream

Directions:

- Set the oven's temperature to 350. Two 8-inch round cake pans should be floured and buttered before any extra flour is shaken out.
- Combine the salt, baking soda, and flour in a sizable bowl.
- Using an electric mixer, beat the butter and sugar in a big bowl until they were frothy and light. One egg at a time is beaten into the mixture, and then almond extract is added (if used). Continue mixing at a low

speed until the dough comes together into a ball. After that, fold in 1/2 cup of the chocolate chips and scrape down the bowl's edges.

- A toothpick inserted in the centre should come out clean after 35 minutes of baking. After cakes have cooled in the pans for five minutes, invert them onto a wire rack to finish cooling.Make the frosting while the cakes are chilling. In a big basin, blend the ricotta using an electric mixer. Add the zests, salt, and cinnamon after that. The mixture should be thoroughly smoothed out before adding the confectioners' sugar. The heavy cream should be whipped for three to four minutes with a whisk attachment to make it thick and firm. Until you're ready to serve it, keep it in the refrigerator.

- The cakes should be separated into four layers horizontally. Place one layer of the cake on four strips of wax paper or parchment paper, each three inches wide, and place them around the edge of a serving plate. Add a cup of icing on top.Once you've sandwiched all of your cake layers, it's time to frost your cake's top portion and sides.

- Gently press the remaining 1/2 cup of chocolate chips, pistachios, and cannoli shells onto the sides of the cake.Wait until you're ready to serve before putting it in the fridge.

27. Cranberry Swirl Cheesecake

Preparation Time:

40 mins

Total Time:

1 hrs 40 mins

Servings:

2 to 3 servings

Ingredients:

- 1/2 a cup of cranberries
- Frozen raspberries, half a cup
- 1 teaspoon orange zest, grated
- Orange juice, 1/4 cup
- 1 cup of sugar, granulated
- One-fourth cup unsalted butter
- 3 containers of cream cheese
- 1 package of chocolate wafer cookies
- 3/4 cups of sour cream
- 3 large eggs
- 2 tablespoons of all-purpose flour
- 2 teaspoons of pure vanilla extract

Directions:

- In a medium saucepan, combine the cranberries, raspberries, orange zest, juice, and 1/4 cup sugar. Heat thoroughly.The cranberries will explode, and the sauce will concentrate in about 5 to 7 minutes of simmering with occasional stirring. A food processor should be used to purée the mixture. After 10 minutes of cooling, store in the fridge until required.
- The oven should be preheated to 375 degrees Fahrenheit. Melt butter and stream it into a 9-inch springform pan. Make sure the food processor is completely dry before using it. Make crumbs by grinding the chocolate wafers. Pulse to incorporate the melted butter after adding it. A toothpick placed in the centre of the cake should come out clean after 35 minutes of baking at 350 degrees. Bake the crust for 10 to 12 minutes, or until it is aromatic and golden brown. Cool before serving on a wire rack. Reduce the oven's heat to no more than 325 degrees Fahrenheit.
- While the crust cools, combine cream cheese and the remaining 3/4 cup sugar in a large bowl and beat with an electric mixer until creamy. Beat until smooth after adding each egg one at a time. In a another bowl, place the remaining half of the filling.Wait until the crust has cooled before adding the remaining filling.

- After adding the reserved filling, dollop generous amounts of the cranberry mixture over the cheesecake batter. To make ornamental swirls, use a table knife to cut through the basic filling with the cranberry batter.
- Bake the cheesecake for 45 to 50 minutes, or until the borders are set but the centre still jiggles a little. Overnight or for around 4 hours, let the cheesecake cool, loosely covered, after removing it from the pan.

28.   Strawberry Rhubarb Layer Cake

Preparation Time:

25 mins

Total Time:

1 hrs 35 mins

Servings:

16 servings

Ingredients:

- Orange, 1
- 3 1/2 cups of sugar, granulated
- 2 pounds of rhubarb
- 1 pound of strawberries
- 4 large egg yolks
- 2 large eggs
- 1 cup of whole milk
- 3 teaspoons of vanilla extract
- 3 cups of cake flour
- 1 tablespoon of baking powder
- 1/2 teaspoon salt
- One pound of butter
- Confectioners' sugar, 1 1/4 cup
- 2 cups heavy cream
- 8 ounces of cream cheese

Directions:

- The orange juice should be poured into a 4-quart kettle. 2 cups of granulated sugar should be added. Cook the mixture, stirring periodically, until the sugar melts. Rhubarb is added, and it is cooked for an additional 5 minutes while stirring. Put the rhubarb in a bowl of ice water to cool it. Uncovered, chill for two hours. After including the sliced strawberries, refrigerate.

- Your oven should be about 350 degrees Fahrenheit hot. Grease three 8-inch cake pans and line them with parchment paper. Spraying and flouring the pan sides and parchment is recommended.

• In a medium bowl, combine the egg yolks, whole eggs, 1/4 cup milk, and 2 teaspoons vanilla and whisk until thoroughly combined. Mix the remaining 1 1/2 cups of granulated sugar and salt with the flour and baking powder in a large bowl on medium-high speed until smooth. Add the egg mixture in three batches, beating thoroughly after each addition. Distribute the batter among the prepared pans in an equal amount. After baking for 20 to 30 minutes, a toothpick inserted into the centre of each cake should come out clean. The cakes should cool on a wire rack for 10 minutes before being turned over to finish cooling.

- Place a cake on a serving dish. After that, drain the liquid from the rhubarb and throw it away. Leave a 1-inch border all the way around the cake's edge. With the second cake and the remaining rhubarb, move on to step two. Incorporate the third cake on top.
- In a large bowl, combine all the ingredients and process with a high-speed blender or food processor until the mixture is smooth. While whisking at high speed, sprinkle in the cream slowly.
- Garnish the cake with sliced berries and a layer of frosting. You have the option of serving it straight away or storing it in the refrigerator for up to a day by wrapping it in plastic wrap.

29.   Abominable Snowman Cake

Preparation Time:

20 mins

Total Time:

2 hrs

Servings:

12 servings

Ingredients:

- Two 8-inch vanilla cake layers
- 1 3/4 cups of bittersweet frosting
- Three tablespoons of purple sanding sugar
- ten purple spice drops
- one marshmallow
- eight blue gum sticks
- a recipe Frosting with marshmallows
- 2 mini chocolate-covered mints
- 10 blue banana-shaped hard candies
- 1 tbsp. blue decorating sugar

Directions:

- Place the bottom of a cake layer on the work surface. Prepare a frosting made with bittersweet chocolate. On top of the cake, spread 1 cup of chocolate frosting. The last cake layer should be positioned with the bottom facing up and gently pressed to adhere.Slice the cake assembly in half along one side, leaving a 2-inch border. Slice the resulting half-length in half again. Cut side down, and place a large cake piece on a platter. Using the wide ends of the trimmed pieces as paws, place them on either side of a giant cake. Before serving, place in the fridge for at least one hour.
- To make the eyes, strew some purple sugar on the work surface.Purple spice drops should be pressed together. Make ovals of spice drops by rolling them out with a rolling pin and adding more sugar to keep them from sticking to the surface. Each flat side of the marshmallow should have an eye cut out of 14 inches. To make 16 teeth, split each stick of gum into two angular triangles.

- Place the remaining 34 cups of chocolate frosting where the eyes and mouth will be on top of the cold cake.On the top third of the cake, place a spice-drop oval horizontally. On the lower third of the cake, poke a toothpick into a 6-by-212-inch oval of the chocolate icing to create a mouth.Take the cake out of the fridge and put it back in.

- Make a marshmallow frosting in the microwave. Divide into two separate resealable plastic bags. Bags should be pressed to remove any extra air before being sealed.

- Cut a 12-inch corner from the frosting-containing bags using a sharp knife.Squeeze, stop, and pull the frosting spikes as you pipe them around the cake, starting at the bottom edge. To cover the cake, pipe rows of piping very close together, avoiding the mouth and eye areas.

- Dots of frosting can be used as eyes for marshmallows. For eyes, use frosting polka dots and crushed mints. All around the opening of the mouth, place cut pieces of gum as teeth. For the claws, use five banana-shaped candies. Sprinkle the sugar with blue food coloring.

THE FROSTING OF DARK CHOCOLATE

- A large bowl should contain 3 cups of confectioners' sugar. Beat 1 cup (2 sticks) of unsalted butter (room temperature) for 2 minutes at medium speed in an electric mixer. Once the mixture is frothy and light, add the 12 tsp. Kosher salt and sugar. 6 ounces of melted bittersweet chocolate, 2 tablespoons heavy cream, and 2 teaspoons pure vanilla essence should be added (cooled).

• Increase the speed to a high setting and beat for several minutes to produce fluffiness.

THE FROSTING OF MARSHMALLOWS

• In a medium saucepan, combine 2 cups sugar, 13 cups light corn syrup, and 12 cups water. Stirring constantly, bring the mixture to a boil until the sugar is completely dissolved.

- When you use an electric mixer, beat 14 cups of Just Whites egg white powder and 12 cups of water for several minutes until foamy and stiff peaks form. The mixture should hold soft peaks after being beaten at high speed for several minutes. While beating, add 2 teaspoons of pure vanilla essence and 2 tablespoons of boiling syrup.Five minutes of beating will result in a smooth, thick, and glossy mixture. Use right away.

30.   Choco-Berry Surprise Cake

Preparation Time:

40 mins

Total Time:

1 hrs

Servings:

20 servings

Ingredients:

FOR CAKE
- Butter without salt for pans
- 2 cups of top-notch, unsweetened cocoa powder plus additional for dusting
- All-purpose flour, 3 cups
- 2.5 cups of sugar, granulated
- Baking soda
- 2 teaspoons of baking powder
- 3 Tbsp. plus 1/4 cup of vegetable oil
- 1 1/4 cup of sour cream
- 1 1/2 cups of hot, strong coffee
- 5 large, beaten eggs
- 1 tablespoon of pure vanilla extract

FOR BUTTERCREAM
- Hull 8 ounces of strawberries
- 3 1/2 sticks of softened unsalted butter
- Confectioners' sugar, 7 cup

FOR THE GLAZE
• 3 ounces of chopped dark chocolate
• 4 tablespoons of salted butter

FOR DECORATING
- Strawberry wholes

Directions:

- Start making it by setting the temperature of your oven to 350 degrees Fahrenheit. Before placing two 8-inch round cake pans in the oven, dust them with cocoa powder. Place parchment paper on the pan bottoms.
- When you have all the ingredients together, make a delicious treat by combining them in a big dish.Combining the above ingredients in one bowl or large container will yield the best results. Whisk together the flour mixture and the wet ingredients until well combined.

- Bake the cakes for 50–55 minutes, or until a toothpick inserted into the centre of the cakes emerges clean. Transfer to a wire rack to finish cooling after five minutes.

Buttercream:

- Slice the strawberries into chunks. Until smooth, mix in a powerful blender or food processor. Set aside at this time. To soften the butter, use an electric mixer. Sift in half of the confectioners' sugar and stir it in gradually. After that, whisk in the strawberry puree and the remaining sugar. Increase the speed to a high setting and beat for an additional 30 seconds until fluffy and light.

- To level the cakes, if necessary, use a serrated knife. Slice each cake horizontally in half to create four layers.Spread about half of the Buttercream between the four layers, ensuring it is evenly distributed. Buttercream should then be applied to the cake's exterior. Before serving, allow for at least 20 minutes of chilling. Put the cake on a board or a cake stand.
- Spread the remaining buttercream on the cake. Reheat in the microwave for a few seconds. While that is going on, make the glaze: The chocolate and butter should be melted together in a heatproof bowl that has been placed over a pan of slightly simmering water.Cool for 5 minutes.

- As you pour the glaze over the chilled, iced cake, allow a few drops to trickle down the sides of the cake.Before garnishing with whole strawberries, Give the cake 15 minutes to cool.

31.   Mini Lemon Blueberry Bundt Cake

Preparation Time:

35 mins

Total Time:

3 hrs and 15 mins

Servings:

16 servings

Ingredients:

- 2 sticks of unseasoned butter, 1 cup
- All-purpose flour, 2 1/2 cups
- 0.5 teaspoons baking soda
- 1/2 teaspoon of kosher salt
- Granulated sugar, 2 cups
- Three big eggs
- One cup of sour cream
- 1 tablespoon lemon zest, grated (from 1 lemon)
- 1 1/3 cups of blueberries, in a 6-ounce package
- Confectioners' sugar, 1 cup
- Lemon juice, 2 tablespoons

Directions:

- Start making it by preheating the oven to 350 degrees Fahrenheit. Use a 12-cup Bundt pan or four 3-cup Bundt pans to butter and flour the pans. In a larger basin, combine the salt, baking soda, and flour.
- For 3 minutes at medium speed, an electric mixer beat the butter and granulated sugar until they were light and fluffy. With the mixer on low, add the eggs at this point. The flour mixture should be combined before adding the sour cream and lemon zest and blending briefly. Beat at high speed for an extra two minutes. Add the blueberries to the combination.
- Bake a 12-cup Bundt pan for 65 to 75 minutes. if a wooden pick inserted into the centre is clean after removal. After the cake has cooled in the pan for 15 minutes, completely invert it onto a cooling rack.
- Whisk the confectioners' sugar and 1 tablespoon of lemon juice together until smooth in a another basin.Just before serving, drizzle the cooled cake with the syrup.

32.　Oatmeal Brownie Bundt Cake

Preparation Time:

40 mins

Total Time:

2 hrs and 30 mins

Servings:

16 servings

Ingredients:

- cooking spray for the pan
- 2 sticks of unsalted butter
- 6 ounces of chopped semisweet chocolate
- 1 cup of almond meal
- 0.5 teaspoons of baking powder
- 0.5 teaspoons baking soda
- Five big eggs
- Confectioners' sugar, 2 cups
- 0.5 cup of chopped nuts (such as almonds)
- 1.5 cups of rolled oats
- Semisweet chocolate chips: 1 cup
- 1/4 cup of heavy cream

Directions:

- Now start by preheating the oven to 350 degrees Fahrenheit a 12-cup Bundt pan should be prepared with cooking spray.
- In a medium bowl that can be microwaved, combine the butter and chocolate chips. Stir the mixture every 30 seconds, and heat on high until chocolate is started to melt and smooth. Cool for 5 minutes.
- In the meantime, combine the baking soda, baking powder, and almond meal in a medium basin.
- Fill an electric mixer with the chocolate mixture, then blend until smooth. One at a time, whip the eggs at a medium-low speed. The almond mixture should be added to a low-speed mixer and blended completely. With sugar, almonds, and oats, make a paste.
- Bake for 45 to 50 minutes, or until nearly clean when tested with a wooden pick inserted close to the middle. Transfer carefully to the prepared pan. Before serving, move the cake to a wire rack and let it cool fully.
- Microwave chocolate chips in 30-second bursts until they start to melt in a tiny bowl that can go in the microwave.Stir until smooth after 15 seconds in the microwave with the cream. Before sprinkling the icing, let the cake cool for 5 to 10 minutes.

33.   Mini Mug Chocolate Cake

Preparation Time:

5 mins

Total Time:

10 mins

Servings:

1 serving

Ingredients:

- 1 tablespoon unsalted butter
- 2 ounces chopped bittersweet chocolate
- 1 big egg
- 2 tablespoons light brown sugar
- 1.5 tablespoons of pure vanilla extract
- 2 tablespoons of all-purpose flour
- 2 tablespoons chocolate powder.
- 0.5 teaspoons of baking powder
- kosher salt pinch
- Whipped topping for serving, such as whipped cream

Directions:

- Allow it cool for five minutes before serving when you've melted In a 10- to 12-ounce round mug, combine the butter and chocolate.
- In the mug, combine the egg, sugar, and vanilla. Mix the flour, cocoa, baking soda, and salt in the mug with a whisk or fork. So now, for about 90 seconds on high in the microwave should be enough to get the center just barely done. If desired, top with whipped cream or other desired garnish.

34. Coconut Cream Cake

Preparation Time:

10 mins

Total Time:

10 mins

Servings:

12 serving

Ingredients:

- Heavy cream, half a point
- Confectioners' sugar: 3 tablespoons
- 1/2 tablespoon coconut extract
- One 8-inch angel food cake from the grocer
- 1 1/4 cups of unsweetened coconut flakes

Directions:

- In a medium bowl, combine heavy cream, confectioners' sugar, and vanilla extract. When lifting the beaters from the bowl of an electric mixer, you should see gentle peaks.
- On a serving plate, flip the cake over. Spread whipped cream over the cake with an offset spatula.
- Spread the coconut-flavored whipped cream over top using your fingertips. Chill for up to one day or serve right away.

35.   Santa Cake

Preparation Time:

35 mins

Total Time:

1 hrs

Servings:

20 serving

Ingredients:

<u>**For Cake**</u>
- All-purpose flour, 2 cups
- Unsweetened cocoa, 1/4 cup
- 1 tablespoon baking soda
- 0.5 teaspoons of baking powder
- Kosher salt, 1/2 teaspoon
- 1 1/2 cups of sugar, granulated
- 1 tablespoon red liquid food dye
- Pure vanilla extract, 1 teaspoon
- 2 tablespoons white vinegar
- 1 1/2 sticks of room temperature, 3/4 cup unsalted butter
- Two big eggs
- One cup of buttermilk

<u>**Frosting**</u>
- 1 1/2 sticks of room temperature, 3/4 cup unsalted butter
- One 8-ounce container of room temperature cream cheese
- One pound of confectioners' sugar

<u>**Decoration**</u>
- 3 chocolate wafer cookies
- cornstarch for the top
- red gel food colouring
- white fondant
- gold food colouring spray
- black fondant are the ingredients

Directions:

<u>**To bake a cake:**</u>

- Set the oven to 350 degrees Fahrenheit before beginning to prepare it. A 13 x 9-inch cake pan should first be lightly oiled before being lined with parchment paper and oiling the parchment as well.
- In a larger basin, combine the flour, cocoa, salt, baking soda, and baking powder. To make it frothy and light, beat all the ingredients with an electric mixer for about 3 minutes. Beat in the eggs one at a time.
- Lower the mixer's speed to low, add the flour mixture and buttermilk in turns, and stir everything together.
- When a toothpick inserted in the centre of the cake comes out clean, bake for 30 to 35 minutes. Prior to transferring to a wire rack to finish cooling, give the food 15 minutes to cool in the pan.

Making the frosting:

• Using an electric mixer, blend the butter and cream cheese until they are completely smooth. Confectioners' sugar is added, and it is frothy after 2 minutes of medium speed beating.

• Fill a sizable piping bag with a flat tip with 1 cup of frosting. The entire cooled cake should be covered with the crimson icing. For five to ten minutes, chill.

Decorate:

- Using the remaining frosting, pipe a strip 3 inches wide and lengthwise through the centre of the cake. As buttons for the top half of the blouse, place two wafer cookies on top and one on the bottom.Using cornstarch, lightly dusk a clear work surface. Cut a 3-inch square out of white fondant after rolling it out. Cut out the center of the square with a smaller cutter to create a belt buckle. A baking sheet with parchment should be sprayed with gold spray, then let to dry for around 10 minutes.
- Place a 9 x 3-inch rectangle of black fondant between the top two and bottom two buttons of the cake. Belt buckle at the back.

36.   Tree Mendous Gingerbread Cake

Preparation Time:

20 mins

Total Time:

1 hrs 25 mins

Servings:

12 serving

Ingredients:

- All-purpose flour
- 2 teaspoons of ground ginger
- 1 teaspoon of baking soda
- 1 teaspoon of ground cinnamon
- 3 cups
- 1/2 teaspoon of ground allspice
- ½ teaspoon. nutmeg, ground
- 1/2 teaspoon salt
- 1/4 teaspoon crushed cloves
- 1/4 teaspoon black pepper, ground
- 1 and a half sticks of softened 3/4 c. butter
- 1 1/2 cups of sugar, granulated
- 2 large eggs
- 1 cup molasses
- 1 teaspoon vanilla essence andconfectioners' sugar for sprinkling

Directions:

- A 350°F oven works best. A 9-inch springform pan should be butter and floured.
- Combine the flour, baking soda, cinnamon, allspice, nutmeg, salt, and pepper in a separate bowl; put this aside.
- Using a mixer set to high, whip the butter and sugar until creamy, about 3 minutes; scrape down the bowl as needed. Reduce your speed to a more bearable rate.Make sure to beat thoroughly after each addition of an egg before moving on to the next one.
- In a measuring cup or medium bowl, combine 4 cups of molasses with 1 cup of boiling water. As you add the molasses/flour mixture and butter mixture to the mixer, reduce the speed to low and beat until incorporated.
- After pouring the mixture onto a baking pan that has been generously buttered, air bubbles should be let out. When a toothpick placed into the centre of the cake comes out clean after 45 to 55 minutes, remove the cake from the oven. On a wire rack, let the cake cool in the pan for 15 minutes. By loosening the

borders, you may remove the pan's side. Permit cooling to finish. If you wish to prepare it ahead of time, wrap it twice in plastic wrap and then in foil. It can be kept for up to a month in the freezer. To hasten the defrosting process, refrigerate.

- Sprinkle confectioners' sugar over the whipped cream before serving.

37.   Candy Cane Forest Cake

Preparation Time:

1 hrs

Total Time:

1 hrs

Servings:

12 serving

Ingredients:

• 1 recipe for White Vanilla Frosting
   • 1 recipe for Chocolate Chip Cake
• Candies: broken red starlight mints and different-sized and-shaped candy canes

Directions:

• Follow the recipe for Chocolate Chip Cake to the letter. Two of the layers' domed tops should be trimmed. Then, cover the cut layer with 2/3 cup of White Vanilla Frosting.Use a domed layer on top for the second and final time. Apply the remaining icing on the top and sides.

• Crumbled starlight mints can be used to adorn the edges and a small portion of the sides. Add candy canes to the cake's icing for a festive touch.

38. Aperol Christmas Cake

Preparation Time:

20 mins

Total Time:

20 mins

Servings:

20 serving

Ingredients:

- 175 g butter, plus more to grease
- 500 g raisins
- 500 g sultanas
- 150 g maraschino cocktail cherries
- 150 ml Aperol, plus 1 tbsp. more
- Finely grated zest of 1 orange
- 175 grammes of light-brown, soft sugar
- 1 1/2 tablespoon. each of cinnamon powder and mixed spices
- 200 g self-raising flour
- 3 medium eggs, beaten

Directions:

- Bake at 150ºC (130ºC fans) in the second position of the oven. Grease and line the bottom and sides of an 8-inch round cake pan with parchment paper.
- In a sizable saucepan, combine 150ml of Aperol, 150ml of sultana juice, and 150ml of orange zest. Add extra Aperol to thin out the sauce if you prefer it thicker, but take care not to overcook it. Butter and sugar should be combined with continuous stirring in a small saucepan set over medium-low heat to melt the sugar.
- Allow cooling for five minutes after removing from heat. The flour and beaten eggs should be incorporated into the mixture. When the batter is done, stream it into the prepared pan and level it up with a spatula.
- 1 hour 45 minutes to 2 hours should be enough time for the cake to be made baking, and a skewer in the middle came out unharmed. If it is browning too soon, wrap the cake with foil.
- Make a few holes in the top of the cooked cake using a cocktail stick.Distribute the final 1 tbsp of Aperol evenly over the top. Utilizing a piece of aluminum foil, cover the cake loosely, and let it finish cooling in the pan. After the dessert has been decorated or served, remove the tin from the freezer.

39. White Christmas cake

Preparation Time:

5 mins

Total Time:

10 mins

Servings:

1 serving

Ingredients:

- Four big eggs, divided
- 0.5 cup of water
- 1 cup softened butter
- 2 cups sugar
- 4 ounces of minced white candy coating
- 1 tablespoon vanilla extract
- 2-and-a-half cups of all-purpose flour
- A half-teaspoon of baking powder
- One-half tsp. baking soda
- 1 cup buttermilk
- 1 cup sweetened coconut shreds
- 1 cup pecans, chopped

Frosting:

- 1 package (8 ounces) softened cream cheese
- 1/2 cup softened butter
- 3-and-a-half cups of confectioners' sugar
- 1 teaspoon vanilla extract
- 1 tablespoon 2% milk

Optional decorations:

- Melted white candy coating or white baking chips
- Red Sixlets candies and sprinkles

Directions:

- Before using, let the egg whites sit at room temperature for 30 minutes.
- Heat a little water to a boil in a small saucepan. Combine with candy coating after being taken off the heat.Cool for 20 minutes.

- Set the oven's temperature to 350 °F. Three 8 or 9-inch round baking pans should be lined with parchment paper that has been greased.
- To achieve a light and fluffy texture, combine the butter and sugar and beat them both for 5-7 minutes. Combine and smooth out with an electric mixer. Add the vanilla and egg yolks. After that, stir in the candy coating mixture. Then, gradually add the flour mixture to the creamed mixture, mixing after each addition of buttermilk until the batter is smooth. In a separate dish, combine the flour, baking powder, and baking soda. Incorporate the coconut and pecans before adding. When stiff peaks form, whip the egg whites on medium speed before folding them into the batter.
- Spread the batter evenly over the pans. Bake for 25 to 30 minutes, or until an inserted toothpick comes out clean near the middle. Discard parchment paper and allow to cool in pans for 10 minutes before transferring to wire racks. Permit cooling to finish.
- Blend the cream cheese and butter together until the frosting is smooth. Add the milk, vanilla essence, and sugar. Smooth a thin layer to the cake's top and edges after adding it to the centre.
- Candy coating can be piped in the shape of leaves and then set in the refrigerator to harden. Sprinkles, foliage, and Sixlets can be used to decorate the cake.

40. Christmas Cookie Cake

Preparation Time:

25 mins

Total Time:

45 mins

Servings:

10 serving

Ingredients:

- 3/4 cup (1 + 1/2 sticks, or 12 TBSP) unsalted butter
- One-third cup of light brown sugar (150 grams)
- 1/4 cup sugar in granules (50 grams)
- 2 cups of unbleached all-purpose flour (240 grammes)
- 1 large egg
- 2 teaspoons of pure vanilla extract
- 2 teaspoons of cornstarch
- 1 teaspoon of baking soda
- 0.5 tsp. of salt
- 3/4 cup chocolate chips, either bittersweet or semisweet

VANILLA BUTTERCREAM FROSTING
- 3/4 cup (1 + 1/2 sticks, or 12 TBSP) unsalted butter
- 3 cups of powdered sugar
- 2 teaspoons of pure vanilla extract plus additional to taste
- 3 TBSP milk
- green and red gel food coloring as needed
- holiday sprinkles for decorating

Directions:

- A large egg is also needed for this step. Before baking, it's essential to let the butter soften and the cold ingredients warm up to room temperature. Preparation is vital when it comes to baking.
- Prepare the dish and preheat the oven to 350 degrees Fahrenheit.
- The first step is making the cookie cake. Using an electric hand mixer, beat the softened butter, brown sugar, and granulated sugar in a big basin until it becomes smooth and creamy.
- Using a mixer, thoroughly integrate the egg and vanilla into the batter.
- In a another basin, mash together the flour, cornstarch, baking soda, and salt.
- Slowly pour the flour mixture into the bigger bowl while continuing to beat on low.
- After the dough has been well incorporated, stir in the chocolate and peanut butter chips.

- To prevent sticking, line the bottom and sides of a springform pan with parchment paper.
- Press your dough onto the pan and bake for 18 to 22 minutes in the centre of the oven. My normal time is 20 minutes since I like a softer centre. Switch your oven to broil on high while your cookie cake bakes and keep an eye on it.Once the golden brown top has browned to perfection, the soft, cookie dough-like center will remain. Remove the food from the oven using oven mitts.
- Allow the cookie cake to cool fully before frosting or slicing. When the cake is first baked, it will be quite soft, but as it cools, it will firm.

To create the frost, follow these steps:

- Use an electric hand mixer to whisk softened butter until it is creamy to produce the buttercream frosting.
- Add the powdered sugar and blend three times, until the mixture is frothy and well combined.
- Add milk to thin the frosting to your preferred consistency by beating in vanilla extract. My 3 TBSP was enough.Add the milk and continue beating for a further 3–4 minutes or until smooth.

A WREATH TO BE MADE:

- 1/4 cup of the icy batter should be set aside for the berries divide it in half to make the light green swirls, and then use the other half to cover the darker green areas of the wreath.
- The frosting can be colored with gel food coloring. Wreaths with red berries and light and dark green frosting are available.
- Spread the green frosting into rows with a small silicone spreader/spatula, then transfer to a piping bag with a French star or large star tip attached.To create a wreath-like design on the cookie cake, green pipe frost around the edges and twist and turn as needed. Fill a small Ziploc bag or piping bag with red frosting and use it to pipe the berries on top of the cake. Simply cut the end of the nozzle and pipe it onto the wreath. Sprinkles are an option.

41.   Pomegranate Christmas cake

Preparation Time:

2 hrs

Total Time:

2 hrs s 30 mins

Servings:

15 serving

Ingredients:

- 6 large eggs, room temp
- 1 cup of sugar
- 1 cup all-purpose unbleached flour
- 0.5 teaspoon baking powder
- 1/2 teaspoon of vanilla extract

For Pomegranate Topping:
- 3/4 cup or 6 ounces of pomegranate juice (Pom Wonderful)
- 2 teaspoons powdered unflavored gelatin. I bought Knox products
- A teaspoon of vanilla extract
- Sugar, two tablespoons
- One large pomegranate's seeds, around 1 1/4 to 1 1/2 cups

For syrup:
- 1 1/2 cups POM brand pomegranate juice
- Two tablespoons of sugar
- Ingredients for the frosting made with pomegranate juice:
- 3 cups of powdered sugar
- 2 sticks of unsalted butter
- 1/4 teaspoon of fine sea salt
- 16 ounces of cream cheese, divided into two blocks, softened at room temperature
- Pomegranate juice, 4 tablespoons

Directions:

- Make sure your oven is preheated to 350 degrees Fahrenheit. Line the bottoms of two 9-inch cake pans with parchment paper to prepare them.
- In a mixing bowl, combine 6 eggs and 1 cup sugar. Beat on high speed for 12 minutes, or until the mixture has tripled in volume and is fluffy.A tablespoon of baking powder is mixed with 1 cup of flour and then sifted into beaten eggs in two additions, with a spatula being used to fold it all in. Blend in half a teaspoon

of vanilla. Remember that the cake's rise depends on the air-infused batter's fluffiness. Your cake will not rise properly if you over-mix it.

- Prepare two 8-inches round cake pans, butter them, and before adding the batter, line them with parchment paper.
- Bake for 25 to 28 minutes, or until the top is golden brown and a toothpick inserted comes out clean, in a 350 degree Fahrenheit oven. Cakes that have cooled on wire racks are ready to be taken from the pans.

The syrup for soaking the cake layers is easy to make:

1 1/2 cups of pomegranate juice and 2 teaspoons of sugar should be combined. Wait for the sugar to dissolve before giving it a few good stirs.

The Frosting Process:

- In a stand mixer equipped with the whisk attachment, combine 2 sticks of butter, 3 cups of powdered sugar, and salt on low speed (1 min). When the mixture becomes light and fluffy, up the speed to medium-high and continue beating it (2 min).
- Add the cream cheese a bit at a time, blending after each addition. This is one after the other; I didn't wait more than three seconds between them. The cream cheese should be incorporated entirely at this point. Beat for another minute.
- Add 4 Tbsp POM juice, 1 Tbsp at a time, and combine (1 min). Until you're ready to use it, keep the frosting in the refrigerator.

Putting your Cake Together:

- By splitting the layers, you can create four layers of cake. Place the first layer on your serving platter with the sliced side facing up. Use a brush to evenly spread a quarter of the POM/sugar syrup over the top of the initial layer. Add an icing coating on top. Count your way through the four layers. The topmost top of the cake just needs a tiny bit of frosting because it will be covered in a Pomegranate glaze.
- Frost the cake's sides after removing any remaining syrup. I used a Wilton 1M star tip in a large size. The ideal border would include a substantial amount of pomegranate topping.
- Before using, the pomegranate topping needs to be chilled for at least 30 minutes.

Adding pomegranate as a garnish:

• Mix 3/4 cup POM juice, 1 teaspoon vanilla essence, and 2 teaspoons of gelatin in a small pot; let rest for 1 minute to soften the gelatin before heating the mixture.

• Add 2 Tbsp. of sugar to a medium skillet, stir regularly, and heat until the sugar melts.

- Removing the saucepan from the heat and placing it in another the next step is to add more cold water to a larger bowl and stir it slowly until it is chilly and somewhat thickened but not set. Utilize your time wisely and be persistent. It has been drained of its ice.
- As soon as the cake has cooled, scatter the pomegranate seeds over it. Once the icing is stiff, keep the cake in the refrigerator (about 1 hour).

42.   Christmas Rum Cake

Preparation Time:

30 mins

Total Time:

1 hrs 30 mins

Servings:

10 to 12 serving

Ingredients:

FOR THE CAKE:
- 1 box of yellow cake mix (approximately 18 oz.)
- One 3.5-ounce bag of instant vanilla pudding mix
- 4 eggs, whole
  - cup of cold water
  - Half a cup canola oil
  - 1/2 cup rum (dark or light is fine)
  - 1 cup brown sugar with chopped pecans (optional)

FOR THE GLAZE:
- 1 and a half sticks of butter
- 1/4 cup of water
- 1 1/2 cups of sugar, granulated
- 3/4 cup rum

Directions:

For the cake:

- Set the oven's temperature to 325 degrees Fahrenheit.
- Flour and spray a bundt cake pan before using it. Top the pan with a layer of nuts.Add a few tablespoons of brown sugar to the nuts if desired.
- Make a cake by combining all the ingredients. Put nuts on top of the batter before pouring it into the pan until the top is even, and sand it down to a smooth finish. Bake for an hour, or even less if the pan is already black. Do not overcook.

When it comes to making the glaze, simply follow these directions:

- Make the glaze while the cake is still 10 minutes in the oven. Butter should be melted in a pot. Add sugar and water and stir well. Bring to a boil for 4 to 5 minutes while stirring continuously. After adding the rum, turn off the heat.For 30 seconds, combine and reheat.
- Let the cake cool after being baked. Immediately drizzle a third of the glaze over the cake's base (top).Allow it to rest for five minutes.
- On a serving platter, flip the cake over. Prick the surface a hundred times with a fork (gently, please.) Drizzle the leftover rum glaze over the top of the cake, letting it run down the edges.Before serving, allow come to room temperature to allow the glaze to absorb fully. Eat. Enjoy. Also, don't feel bad about it. Merry Christmas to you and yours!

43.   Chocolate-Covered Cheesecake Trees

Preparation Time:

1 hrs 10 mins

Total Time:

5 hrs 15 mins

Servings:

28 serving

Ingredients:

* 1 cup crumbs from chocolate wafers
* 1/4 cup melted butter or margarine
* 2 softened (8 oz each) packets of cream cheese
* 0.5 cups sugar
* ¼ tablespoon sour cream
* One teaspoon of vanilla
* 2eggs
* 28 flat wooden sticks with round ends or paper lollipop sticks
* Semisweet chocolate chips, 3 1/2 cups (from a 24-oz bag)
* Three teaspoons of shortening
* 2 ounces of chopped vanilla-flavored almond bark candy coating
* A half-spoon of vegetable oil

Directions:

* Set the temperature of the oven to 300 degrees Fahrenheit. Use heavy-duty foil to cover the sides of an 8-inch pan. Butter and wafer crumbs are put in a small basin. Indent the pan's foil-lined bottom.
* The cream cheese and sugar are smoothed out in a big bowl using an electric mixer. Sour cream, vanilla, and eggs have all been added. Pour the crust on top.

* Bake the dish for 30 to 40 minutes, or until the filling is bubbling and the edges have browned.30 minutes of cooling on a cooling rack in the pan. After covering the container, freeze it for two hours. Wax paper 1 large cookie sheet in the interim.
* To remove the cheesecake from the pan, lift the foil. Four long strips can be cut from the same piece of meat. Work with one long piece at a time, cutting each piece into seven triangles. Place the sticks in the bottoms of the triangles. Spread the dough out on a cookie sheet that has been lined with wax paper. In the freezer for 30 minutes. Freeze until ready to coat with chocolate if making and covering and freezing until ready.

- In a 2-quart saucepan over low heat, melt the chocolate chips and shortening while stirring continuously. All of the ingredients should be combined in a medium bowl.

- Quickly dip each tree into the melted chocolate using a spatula, letting the extra drip off. Work in two batches of 14 at a time. Spread chocolate around the stick's opening with a knife or spatula. Waxed paper, crust side down, should be placed on a baking sheet.

- In a small microwave-safe bowl, combine candy coating and oil; microwave on High for 1 minute, stirring every 15 seconds till it completely melted. Add food coloring to the mixture. Place in a 1-quart resalable plastic bag for food storage. The bag's corner should be cut out and sealed. Trees were draped with a garland-like coating of pipe melted. Frozen food should be protected from light and kept at a consistent temperature.

44. Applesauce Cake

Preparation Time:

15 mins

Total Time:

2 hrs 30 mins

Servings:

12 serving

Ingredients:

FOR THE CAKE:
- Flour-based nonstick baking spray
- 2 1/2 c. universal flour
- 1 1/2 tsp. bread soda
- 1/2 tsp. a baking soda
- ½ teaspoon. Salt
- 2 teaspoons. nutmeg in apple pie
- 1 cup refined sugar
- 1 cup sugar, light brown, in bags
- 1 1/2 cup granular applesauce
- 1/2 cup oil from plants
- 1/2 cup milk
- Two big eggs
- 2 tablespoons. vanilla essence
- 3/4 c. chopped walnuts, optional, plus more for garnish

FOR THE FROSTING:
- Two butter sticks
- 3 1/2 cup. granulated sugar
- 1/3 cup maple sugar
- 1 teaspoon. vanilla essence
- 1/4 tablespoon. salt
- 1/3 cup thick cream

Directions:

For the cake:

• Set the oven's thermostat to 350 degrees Fahrenheit. A 9-by-13-inch baking pan should be coated with flour and nonstick baking spray.

• In a sizable basin, whisk together the baking soda, baking powder, salt, cinnamon, nutmeg, and brown sugar. The mixture of oil, milk, eggs, and vanilla essence should be added. Just enough time to guarantee that all the ingredients are thoroughly mixed. If desired, incorporate the walnuts.

- For 35-40 minutes, bake the cake at 350 degrees Fahrenheit until only a few moist crumbs are removed from the center when a toothpick is inserted. The cake can cool on a wire rack for one to twelve hours.

The icing on the cake:

- Once the froth and butter beneath it have turned golden brown, continue to cook the butter in a medium skillet over medium heat, stirring regularly. Add a few swirls of the heatproof bowl to stop the browning. While the cake bakes and cools, allow it to cool entirely at room temperature, about 2 hours.
- Cream up the butter using a hand mixer and smooth, scraping the sides of the bowl as necessary. Set aside to cool completely before using. Over medium-high heat, gently bring all the ingredients in a medium saucepan to a boil. Beat for two minutes at medium speed until fluffy and light. You can garnish the dish with more walnuts if you prefer. Slice and serve right now, or put it in the fridge until you need it.

45. Hummingbird Coffee Cake

Preparation Time:

10 mins

Total Time:

55 mins

Servings:

9 serving

Ingredients:

Browned Butter:
- a half cup of unsalted butter

Streusel Topping:
- One-third cup all-purpose flour
- A quarter cup tightly packed brown sugar
- 1/2 teaspoon cinnamon powder
- 1/4 tablespoon. Salt
- 3 ½ tablespoons unsalted butter, softened
- ½ cup pecans, chopped

Cake:
- Two big eggs
- 1 mashed big banana
- ½ cup drained pineapple chunks
- 1 teaspoon vanilla extract
- 1 ½ cups all-purpose flour
- ¾ cup granulated sugar
- ¼ cup brown sugar, firmly packed
- ¾ teaspoon salt
- ¾ teaspoon baking powder
- ½ teaspoon ground cinnamon

Glaze Topping:
- ½ cup powdered sugar
- 2 tablespoons sour cream
- 1 ½ teaspoons milk

Directions:

- 350 degrees Fahrenheit in the oven is the ideal temperature for baking. The 8-inch square baking dish needs to be lightly dusted and coated with cooking spray. Get rid of.

- In a medium saucepan over medium heat, melt half a cup of butter until it turns golden brown and smells nutty.
- To cool down, remove it from the heat source.
- Combine well in a small bowl the flour, brown sugar, cinnamon, and salt. Add the 3 12 tablespoons softened butter until crumbly and then the 12 cup pecans. Dispose of.
- Using a paddle attachment on a stand mixer, combine the 2 large eggs with the 1 large banana, 12 cups of crushed pineapple, till completely blended. add 1 teaspoon of vanilla extract. Continue mixing until the 12-cup browned butter is incorporated.
- All-purpose flour; 34 cups granulated sugar; 14 cups brown; 3/8 teaspoon salt; 3/8 teaspoon Separately, combine the baking powder with the 1/8 teaspoon of ground cinnamon in a small bowl.
- Mix thoroughly after each addition while adding the flour mixture one tablespoon at a time on low speed.
- Half of the streusel mixture should be spread over the bottom of the prepared baking pan before being covered. 12 of the cake mixture should be distributed on top.
- Top the cake batter with the remaining streusel mixture, and bake as directed.
- A cake tester should come clean after 40 to 45 minutes of baking at 350 degrees Fahrenheit. Take out of the oven and let cool in the pan on a cooling rack for 10 to 15 minutes. By running a knife around the cake's edge, you can get the cake out of the pan.
- This recipe calls for whisking together 1 cup powdered sugar, 2 TBS sour cream, and 1 12 TBS milk. Drizzle the frosting evenly over the top of the warm cake.

46.   Eggnog Pound Cake

Preparation Time:

5 mins

Total Time:

10 mins

Servings:

1 serving

Ingredients:

POUND CAKE
- 1 16oz box pound cake mix
- 1 ¼ cups egg nog
- 3 large eggs
- ¼ cup softened butter, unsalted
- 1/2 tablespoon. Nutmeg
- A teaspoon of vanilla extract
- 1/2 lemon zest

ICING
- Sugar for confections, 1 1/2 cups
- A dash of salt
- 1/4 teaspoon vanilla extract
- 1 tablespoon melted unsalted butter
- 7-8 teaspoons of milk

Directions:

- A 350°F oven is ideal.
- Pour the cake mix from the package into a mixing basin. Blend in nutmeg.
- Prior to incorporating them into the dish containing the cake mix, combine the remaining ingredients in a different basin. Blend the ingredients until they are entirely smooth.
- You can line a pan with parchment paper or bake a loaf in a greased and floured pan. Pour the batter and give it a light shake to level it.
- Bake the cake for 40 minutes at least, or until a toothpick put into it comes out clean.
- Let the cake cool fully before frosting.

- **FOR ICING**

- Butter, vanilla, sugar, and salt are combined in a small basin.

- Add 2 teaspoons of milk until it reaches a drizzleable consistency.

47.   Christmas Saguaro cactus Cake

Preparation Time:

2 hrs

Total Time:

8 hrs

Servings:

5 to 6 servings

Ingredients:

For the Meringues
- 170 grammes egg whites - about 4 large eggs
- 100 grammes superfine sugar
- 60 grammes of sugar in powder
- Salt, 1/4 teaspoon
- 3/4 teaspoon of vanilla extract
- Food colouring in green
- Black Royal Icing
- Mixed color dragees

For the Cake
- 3/4 cup buttermilk
- 2/3 C sour cream
- 1 teaspoon of vanilla extract
- 4 egg whites
- 1/3 cup of vegetable oil
- White cake mix, 1 box
- Food Coloring Gel
- For the Buttercream
- 2 cups butter
- 6 cups of granulated sugar
- 0.5 tablespoon. of salt
- 0.5 cups thick cream
- 1 teaspoon of vanilla extract
- Food Coloring

Directions:

The Meringues are ready to be made:

- Set the oven temperature to 175F. Use parchment paper or a silicone mat to cover two large cookie sheets. NEVER EVER pipe on an unlined cookie sheet! THEY WILL REMAIN!
- Using the whisk attachment on a stand mixer, beat the egg whites until frothy.
- Stir thoroughly after each addition as you add the superfine sugar, one tablespoon at a time. Add the extract just before finishing the whipping on medium-high speed till the stiff peaks form.
- Use a sifter to mix the salt and granulated sugar in a big bowl. Add the granulated sugar to the eggs.
- Attach a Popsicle stick to a dot of meringue on the cookie sheet. Put on the cactus shape with a large 1M piping tip in a pastry bag.
- Four hours in the oven. At the two-hour mark, rotate the cookie sheets.
- Baked meringues should be left in the oven overnight to dry out completely. They do not need to be used right away; you may keep them warm in the oven.
- **Cakes are ready to be baked:**
- Set the oven to 325ºF. Using flour and nonstick spray, prepare six 6-inch cake pans. Get rid of.
- The sour cream, egg whites, extract, and vegetable oil should be combined in a sizable basin. Cake mix should be incorporated into the batter (do NOT just dump it in).
- Mix until everything is evenly distributed.
- Just the white cake mix should be used in one cake pan. Gradually incorporate blue and green food coloring into each cake layer to achieve an ombre effect.
- The cake layers should be baked for 20 minutes. Remove it from the oven and place it on a cooling rack.
- To get the best frosting results, place the cake layers in the freezer overnight after wrapping them in plastic.

To prepare the Buttercream:

- Use a paddle attachment on your stand mixer to beat the butter for 4 minutes, or until it is frothy and light.
- Once the butter is creamy, add sugar and salt, one tablespoon at a time, after they have been properly sifted.
- Gradually blend in the heavy cream, vanilla extract, and food colorings until the appropriate level of green, orange, and red is achieved. It will get darker as time passes, so be careful with your lighting. Until needed, store under cover in a cool, dry area.

Decorate a cake:

- Take the cakes out of the freezer and let them thaw. Place the darkest cake on top of a dollop of butter on a cardboard cake round. Repeat the cake and buttercream layering adding 1/4 cup of the Buttercream on top to complete. After the cake is frosted, it should be refrigerated for 15 minutes before serving.
- Add a second layer of Buttercream to the cake and use a cake scraper to smooth the edges. A lip around the cake's perimeter can be achieved by allowing the edge of the cake to be left unfinished.
- Crush graham crackers and sprinkle them on top of the cake before serving.
- Using some frosting, decorate the cake's edge with cacti-shaped meringue flowers, then insert lollipop sticks to hold them.

48.   Grasshopper Cake

Preparation Time:

20 mins

Total Time:

47 mins

Servings:

20 serving

Ingredients:

FOR THE CAKE:
- One box of Betty Crocker Super Moist White Cake Mix that includes pudding
- 1-1/4 cups of water
- Vegetable oil, 1/3 cup
- 4 ounces of Creme de Menthe liqueur or syrup
- 3 egg whites from 3 large eggs

FOR THE TOPPING:
- One (16-ounce) jar of hot fudge topping
- 1 8-oz. Cool Whip container
- Creme de Menthe, 2 oz
- optional chopped Andes Mint garnish

Directions:

- Set the oven to 350°F for glossy metal or glass pans or 325°F for dark or nonstick pans. Only gently cover the bottom of a 9" x 13" baking pan with nonstick spray.
- Add the ingredients to a sizable mixing basin, and beat with an electric mixer on low speed for 30 seconds. Increasing the mixer speed to medium, beat for two minutes while occasionally scraping down the bowl. There will be some chunks in the batter. The Creme de Menthe should be added. The batter should be poured into the heating pan.
- After baking for 27 to 32 minutes, a toothpick inserted in the center should come out clean. If you overbake it, you'll get a dry cake. Allow for complete cooling.
- To complete, gently spread the fudge topping over the cake using a spatula. In a medium bowl, combine 2 ounces of creme de Menthe and Cool Whip.
- Evenly distribute the mixture over the fudge. Andes Mints can be used as a garnish if desired. Refrigerate tightly covered.

49.   Snowman Cake

Preparation Time:

15 mins

Total Time:

2 hrs 3 mins

Servings:

16 serving

Ingredients:

Cake

- White Cake Mix, 1 Box
- The recipe on the cake mix box called for water, vegetable oil, and eggs.
- A sizable cardboard tray or tray covered in foil and wrapping paper

Frosting and Decorations

- 1 receptacle Whipped fluffy white frosting
- 1 cup flaked or shredded coconut
- 3 pieces of red shoestring licorice
- 4 semisweet chocolate chips
- 1 large black gumdrop
- 1 large green gumdrop
- 10 large gumdrops total
- 2 cookies with chocolate wafers

Directions:

- Turn the oven's dial to 350 degrees Fahrenheit. Follow the directions on the package for two 8- or 9-inch round cakes, or bake and cool the cake in one 8-inch and one 9-inch round pan.
- Lay out the cake rounds in the pattern shown. Apply a layer of frosting to the cake. Gently press down on the coconut to ensure that it adheres.
- For the nose and brows, use black gumdrops, chocolate chips, and licorice for the mouth, muffler, and chocolate chips, respectively. Attach licorice to the top of the head and place a cookie on each side for earmuffs. Keep covered but not tightly.

50.   Gingerbread Castle Cake

Preparation Time:

45 mins

Total Time:

2 hrs 35 mins

Servings:

12 serving

Ingredients:

- 1 package cake batter
- The recipe on the cake mix box called for water, vegetable oil, and eggs
- 1 cup melted chocolate chips
- Half a cup of cream vanilla frosting
- 4round peppermint candies
- 4peppermint candy sticks
- 1/2cup small gumdrops
- 3spearmint gumdrop leaves
- Edible glitter, if desired

Directions:

- The oven should be preheated to 325 Fahrenheit degrees. A 9-inch round cake pan should be greased and floured baking spray flavored with flour to coat the pan.
- The cake mix box will tell you how to make the batter. Pour the batter into a pan.
- The cake is done baking when a toothpick put in the middle of it comes out clean. 10 minutes to cool. If necessary, trim the cake to the top of the pan with a serrated knife. Turn the pan over and place it on a cooling rack to remove it. Give cooling at least an hour.
- Serve cake on a 12- to 15-inch plate, tray, or foil-wrapped cardboard square. Cut off a tiny corner of a small resealable food-storage plastic bag and place the melted chocolate chips inside. The door and window panes can be outlined with melted chocolate.
- Attach the round candies to the four candy sticks with a small amount of frosting and let them dry. The rest of the frosting can be microwaved and stored in the corner of a small resealable food storage bag. Ten seconds on high in a sealed bag. A small piece of the bag was cut off. Decorate the roof, tower spires, and windows with frosting. Make the castle's roof and sides with gumdrops. Top each tower with a candy stick topped with a round candy; if desired, drizzle the tops with frosting. Bring a couple of spearmint leaves up front. Form a wreath out of the remaining spearmint leaves and attach it to the door with a dab

of frosting. Add candy sprinkles to the wreath and the entrance as desired. To make it appear as if there is snow on top of the castle, dust it with edible glitter. Keep covered but not tightly.

51 Perfect Sugar Cookies

Preparation Time:

15 mins

Total Time:

1 hrs 45 mins

Servings:

2 dozen

Ingredients:

<u>**FOR THE COOKIE DOUGH**</u>
- 3 cups of all-purpose flour + additional for surfaces
- 1 teaspoon baking soda
- 1/2 teaspoon of kosher salt
- 1 cup (2 sticks) softened butter
- 1 cup of sugar, granulated
- 1 big egg
- One teaspoon of vanilla extract
- 1 tablespoon milk

<u>**FOR THE BUTTERCREAM FROSTING**</u>
- 1 cup (2 sticks) softened butter
- Powdered sugar, 5 cups
- 1/4 cup of heavy cream
- Half a teaspoon of almond extract
- 1/4 teaspoon of kosher salt
- Colorants in food

Directions:

- Combine the flour, baking soda, and salt in a sizable bowl before setting it aside.
- In a different, big bowl, beat the butter and sugar until they are light and fluffy. After thoroughly combining the egg, milk, and vanilla essence, add the flour mixture gradually until it is fully integrated.
- Wrap in plastic and refrigerate. 1 hour in the refrigerator.
- Before starting the rolling process, preheat the oven to 350°F and line two baking sheets with parchment paper. On a floured surface, roll out the dough to a thickness of 1/8". Place the shapes on the parchment paper-lined baking sheets. The shapes will hold while baking if you first freeze them for ten minutes.
- Use a hand mixer to thoroughly combine butter and powdered sugar in a large bowl to prepare the frosting. Cream, almond extract, and salt are added by beating.

- Bake cookies for 8 to 10 minutes, or until the edges start to turn brown.
- Make sure it's completely cooled down before frosting and decorating.

52. Gingerbread Cookies

Preparation Time:

15 mins

Total Time:

3 hrs 15 mins

Servings:

25 servings

Ingredients:

- 1 1/2 sticks of softened 3/4 cup butter
- 3/4 cup of brown sugar in a bag
- 2/3 cup of molasses
- 1 big egg
- One teaspoon of vanilla extract
- All-purpose flour, 3 1/4 c. Flour
- 1 tablespoon ginger powder
- 1 tablespoon baking soda
- 1 teaspoon cinnamon, ground
- 0.5 teaspoon ground cloves
- 1/4 teaspoon of ground nutmeg
- 1/2 teaspoon of kosher salt
- A 2" piece of grated fresh ginger (optional)
- zest from one orange (optional)
- A half teaspoon of freshly ground black pepper (optional)
- Icing for adorning sugar cookies
- decorative sprinkles

Directions:

- Using a hand mixer, beat the butter, brown sugar, and molasses in a sizable basin until light and fluffy, about 2 minutes. Continue beating until all ingredients are well-combined.
- In a larger basin, combine the flour, spices, baking soda, and salt. Stir in the fresh ginger, orange zest, and black pepper while mixing on low until the dough just comes together.
- Make two discs by dividing the dough in half. Then put them in the fridge for about 2 to 3 hours until they're solid.
- Line two sizable baking trays with parchment paper and preheat the oven to 350 degrees. On a surface that has been lightly dusted with flour, place one dough disc and roll it out to a thickness of about 1/4 inch. Using the large cookie cutter, create 3D gingerbread men and arrange them on baking sheets.

97

- Depending on the size of the cookie cutters you're using, puff the dough and bake for 9 to 10 minutes. Allow the baked products to cool for five minutes on the baking sheets before transferring them to a cooling rack to finish cooling.
- You can repeat the process with the second disc of dough. As desired, top the cake with icing and sprinkles.

53.   Snowball Cookies

Preparation Time:

15 mins

Total Time:

2 hrs 25 mins

Servings:

2 dozen

Ingredients:

- 1 cup (2 sticks) softened butter
- 1 1/2 cups of split powdered sugar
- 2 cup general purpose Flour
- 1 tablespoon. pure vanilla extract
- 1 cup of chopped walnuts
- 1/2 teaspoon of kosher salt
- Water, 2 tablespoons
- 24 unwrapped chocolate kisses

Directions:

- Set the oven at 325 degrees. Using parchment paper, cover two baking sheets.
- Cream butter and 12 cups powdered huge basin of sugar and a hand mixer be sure to integrate all of the ingredients before you finish.
- Roll each chocolate Kiss in a ball of cookie dough after moulding it around it with a tablespoon. Wait an hour before serving.
- Bake the cookies for just 20 to 25 minutes, or until they are completely dry and lack colour.
- Next, sprinkle the cookies with the final cup of powdered sugar.

54.   Christmas Pinwheel Cookies

Preparation Time:

10 mins

Total Time:

2 hrs 30 mins

Servings:

2 dozen

Ingredients:

- 2 1/4 c. general purpose Flour
- 1 teaspoon baking soda
- 1/2 teaspoon of kosher salt
- 1 cup (2 sticks) softened butter
- 1 cup of sugar, granulated
- 1 big egg
- 3/4 teaspoon of almond extract
- Red food colouring
- Sprinkles

Directions:

- Next, whisk together the flour, baking soda, and salt in a smaller basin before adding them to the batter. Butter and sugar should be mixed together in a big bowl using a hand mixer. Add the extract after adding the egg. Add wet and dry ingredients to a mixing bowl, then beat until combined.
- Split the dough in half, keeping one half in the mixing bowl. Make a small addition of red food colouring and continue mixing until the desired shade is attained. Create a 12" thick square out of each dough piece. Wrapped in plastic, chill for 30 minutes or until stiff.
- Between two pieces of parchment paper, roll the red dough into a 1/4-inch-thick rectangle. Continue with the white dough. Remove the parchment paper top sheet from each dough ball. the white dough should be placed on top of the red dough with the red and white dough's short ends facing each other. Make a light press on the dough's surface to aid in its bonding.

- Removing the top layer of parchment paper and trimming the sides to match up evenly is necessary. Starting with the short end, tightly roll the dough into a log Seal the log's edge by rolling it on the counter several times. Simply cover with plastic wrap, chill for at least an hour, or overnight.

- The oven should be preheated to 350 degrees. Put two large baking sheets together in a row using parchment paper. On a medium plate, spread out the sprinkles. Slice the cookies 1/2" thick with a sharp knife and roll the edges in sprinkles. On baking sheets, space them 2 inches apart.

- Bake for 10 minutes, or until the edges are firm and just starting to brown.

55. Brown Butter Chocolate Cookies

Preparation Time:

10 mins

Total Time:

2 hrs 50 mins

Servings:

20 servings

Ingredients:

2 sticks of butter, 1 cup
1-tablespoon milk powder
3/4 cup of packed brown
Granulated sugar, half a cup
two huge eggs
Pure vanilla extract, 1 teaspoon
All-purpose: 2 1/2 c. Flour
Baking soda, 1 teaspoon
Kosher salt, 1/2 teaspoon
Chocolate chips, 2 cups

Directions:

- In a small skillet or saucepan over medium heat, make a straightforward butter sauce. The butter should be cooked, occasionally stirring, until it simmers. Shortly simmer the butter until it starts to turn golden in colour. Check to see if the butter has developed a rich golden hue give it another stir once it has quieted and stopped sizzling. Scrape the brown bits into a medium heatproof bowl before removing them from the heat. Allow for a 15 to 20-minute cooling period.
- Browned butter is combined with milk powder; whisk until all of the powder is dissolved. Once the eggs and vanilla are creamy, add the sugars and continue whisking.

- In a different medium basin, combine the flour, baking soda, and salt. Stir the dry ingredients into the wet components using a rubber spatula until barely mixed. Add the chocolate chips to the center and make a well there.

- Refrigerate for two hours after wrapping in plastic wrap.
• Line only two sizable baking sheets with parchment paper, then heat the oven to 350 degrees. Utilizing about 2 tablespoons of the mixture, form the dough into a ball. Place on the baking sheets 2" apart.
- Baking time is between 10 and 12 minutes, depending on the thickness of your cookies. Only two large baking sheets should be lined with parchment paper, and the oven should be preheated at 350 degrees.

Form the dough into a ball using about 2 teaspoons of the ingredients. Place 2" apart on the baking sheets.

56. Lofthouse Cookies

Preparation Time:

10 mins

Total Time:

2 hrs 30 mins

Servings:

15 servings

Ingredients:

FOR COOKIES:
- 2 1/4 cups all-purpose flour plus additional flour for surfaces
- 1/4 cup cornstarch
- 1 teaspoon baking soda
- 1 tablespoon kosher salt
- 1/2 cup (1 stick) softened butter
- 4 ounces of softened cream cheese
- 1 cup of sugar, granulated
- 1 big egg
- One teaspoon of vanilla extract
- A teaspoon of almond extract

FOR BUTTERCREAM:
- 1 1/2 sticks of softened 3/4 cup butter
- 2.775 cups of powdered sugar
- One tablespoon thick cream
- One teaspoon of vanilla extract
- A dash of kosher salt
- food colorings
- decorative sprinkles

Directions:

- Combine the Flour, cornstarch, a large basin with salt and baking powder.
- Using a hand mixer, beat the butter, cream cheese, and sugar in a separate big bowl until they are light and fluffy. The pieces and egg should be completely mixed before being added. In a mixing bowl, combine the wet and dry ingredients. Beat well to combine. Make a disc out of the dough by transferring it to plastic wrap and smoothing it out. At this point, the dough will still be soft and sticky.

- Before serving, make sure the food has chilled for at least an hour.
- Reheat the oven to 350°. Put the dough on the counter and dust it with flour. It's important to flour the dough's top as well. Roll out the dough to a thickness of 12". Use a 3" round cookie cutter to make the cookies, and space them 2" apart on the baking sheets. To make more cookies, simply reroll the scraps and cut them again.
- For most satisfactory results, bake for 10 to 12 minutes until the centers are just barely done but the edges are barely set. There shouldn't be many colorations on the top of cookies. Cool completely on baking sheets before moving on to the next step.

- As a side note: To make the frosting, whip the butter using a hand mixer's paddle attachment in a sizable bowl for 2 minutes until it's completely smooth and creamy. Add the powdered sugar, then beat for a further three minutes. heavy cream, beating it in vanilla, and a dash of salt after you've added the other ingredients. Beat in the desired amount of food colorings until well combined.
- Using an offset spatula, Put a thick layer of frosting and sprinkles on top of the cooled cookies.

57. Santa's Trash Cookies

Preparation Time:

15 mins

Total Time:

1 hrs

Servings:

20 servings

Ingredients:

- 1 cup (2 sticks) softened butter
- 1/2 cup of sugar, granulated
- Half a cup of packed brown sugar
- 1 big egg
- Two teaspoons of vanilla extract
- 2 1/4 c. general purpose Flour
- 1 tablespoon baking soda
- 1/4 teaspoon of kosher salt
- 3/4 cup of potato chips, crushed
- 3/4 cup of pretzels, crushed
- Semisweet chocolate chips: 1 1/4 cups
- 1/2 cup of sprinkles in red and green
- To garnish, use flaky sea salt

Directions:

- Row two baking sheets with parchment paper and Set the oven's temperature to 350 degrees. With a hand mixer, beat the butter and sugars in a sizable bowl for three to four minutes, or until they are light and fluffy.
- Egg and vanilla should be incorporated into the mixture.
- Combine the flour, baking soda, and salt in a second big bowl. Just until mixed, whisk the dry and wet ingredients together.
- Gently mix the majority of the chips, pretzels, chocolate chips, and sprinkles into the batter.
- Place 2 tablespoons of dough on each prepared baking sheet using a medium cookie scoop. Each cookie should be flattened slightly before being topped with the remaining chips, pretzels, chocolate chips, and sprinkles. Flaky salt can be added to the dish.
- Until the edges start to brown, bake for 14 minutes.
- Let it sit in the oven for 2 to 3 minutes before removing it and setting it on a cooling rack.

58.   Giant Chocolate Chip Cookies

Preparation Time:

10 mins

Total Time:

2 hrs 30 mins

Servings:

4 servings

Ingredients:

- 1 tablespoon plus 3/4 cup all-purpose flour
- 1 tablespoon plus 3/4 cup cake flour
- 1 teaspoon baking soda
- 1/4 teaspoon of kosher salt
- 1 stick of chilled butter, half a cup
- 1/3 cup of sugar, granulated
- Brown sugar, one-third cup
- A single giant egg with its yolk
- Half a teaspoon of pure vanilla extract
- 3 1/2 c. plus 2 tablespoons chocolate chips
- Flaky sea salt

Directions:

- To prepare, line a large baking sheet with parchment paper, and putting it in the freezer with enough room to accommodate it. simply mux universal Salt, baking powder, cake flour, and flour in a medium bowl.
- Traveling slowly, whip the cold butter in a stand mixer until it loses its shape, about 30 to 40 seconds. Keep creaming for 60 seconds until there are no large butter chunks left.
- Combine and fluffy-up the egg, the egg yolk, and the vanilla extract. The flour mixture should be added gradually until fully integrated. After that, stir in 112 cups of chocolate chips to spread them equally throughout the dough.
- Add the remaining 2 cups of chocolate chips to a medium-sized bowl. A generous 34 cup of dough should be used to portion out large dough balls. Each ball should be rolled in the chips one at a time, leaving the bottom of the bowl untouched. Complete any massive gaps with more chocolate chips and lightly press them into each dough ball.
- Frozen for 90 minutes, Combine and fluffy-up the egg, the egg yolk, and the vanilla extract. The flour mixture should be added gradually until fully integrated. After that, stir in 112 cups of chocolate chips to

spread them equally throughout the dough then top each ball of dough with 12 tablespoons of chocolate chips.

- Bake for 25-30 minutes till it gets golden around the corners but still pale in the center. Before serving, allow cookies to cool completely.

59. Italian Ricotta Cookies

Preparation Time:

15 mins

Total Time:

3 hrs 15 mins

Servings:

25 servings

Ingredients:

FOR THE COOKIES
- 2 cup general purpose Flour
- 1.5 teaspoons of baking powder
- 1/2 teaspoon of kosher salt
- 1/4 cup (1/2 stick) softened butter
- 1 cup of sugar, granulated
- Ricotta, 8 ounces
- One teaspoon of vanilla extract
- 1/2 teaspoon of almond extract (optional)
- 1 egg

FOR THE ICING
- One cup of powdered sugar
- 2 tablespoons whole milk
- 1/4 teaspoon of almond extract (optional)
- Sprinkles

Directions:

Preparation of cookies

• Simply warm your oven to 350 degrees Fahrenheit to begin. Two baking sheets should be covered with parchment paper.

• In a larger basin, combine the flour, baking soda, and salt. Put off till later.

• Using a stand mixer or a large bowl, whip the butter and sugar on medium speed until they are light and fluffy.

• Combine the ricotta cheese, vanilla extract, and any additional flavorings, like almond extract, using an electric mixer.

•You only need to combine the dry ingredients, and you're done.

- Divide the dough into 112 sections the size of tablespoons using a medium cookie scoop, and space them 2 inches apart on the parchment paper. For around 15 minutes, bake. They will have a golden brown bottom and a pale top. A wire tray with parchment paper under the cookies is ideal for cooling them.

The icing on the cookies is to make it:

- Add the milk and powdered sugar to a blender, and blend until smooth. The almond extract can be added at this point if desired. When the icing is still wet, spoon the icing over the cookies and top with sprinkles.

60. Chocolate Crinkles Cookies

Preparation Time:

5 mins

Total Time:

2 hrs 45 mins

Servings:

18 servings

Ingredients:

- 1-and-a-half cups all-purpose flour
- Unsweetened cocoa powder, 3/4 cup
- 1 teaspoon kosher salt
- 1 teaspoon baking soda
  - 3/4 teaspoon of baking soda
  - 1/2 cup (1 stick) melted butter
  - 3/4 cup of sugar, granulated
  - Half a cup of packed brown sugar
  - Three big eggs
  - Rolling sugar in powder

Directions:

- Flour, cocoa powder, salt, baking soda, and baking powder should all be combined in a big bowl.
- Melted butter, sugars, and eggs should be thoroughly combined in a medium bowl. Add dry ingredients after combining wet components barely. Refrigerate for at least two hours, covered with plastic wrap.
- Row just two large baking sheets and set the oven to 350 degrees. Cover with parchment paper. Add powdered sugar to a small bowl and mix it in thoroughly. Form a ball of about 2 tablespoons of dough using your hands. Wet your hands a little to help roll the dough if it is too sticky. Roll the dough into a ball with a rolling pin, then put the balls approximately 2 inches apart on a baking sheet that has been prepared. Roll each piece of dough in powdered sugar once more after you've covered the entire thing. Crinkles will appear more prominently when the cookies are baked this way.
- Cookies should puff and crack after 14 minutes in the oven. The edges will be set, but the cracks will still appear undercooked. Allow cooling entirely on a baking sheet before removing.

61.Gingersnap Cookies

Preparation Time:

5 mins

Total Time:

1 hrs 30 mins

Servings:

16 servings

Ingredients:

• 2 cups all-purpose flour

• 2 teaspoons of ginger powder

• 1 teaspoon of cinnamon

• 1 tablespoon kosher salt

• 0.5 teaspoons baking soda

• 1/4 teaspoon crushed cloves

- Vegetable oil, 1 cup
- 1/3 cup, ideally Grandma's, molasses
- 1 cup of brown sugar in bags
- 2 tablespoons of more sugar for rolling
- 1 big egg
- Pure vanilla extract, 1 teaspoon

Directions:

- This recipe calls for a medium-sized bowl filled with gingerbread spices such as cinnamon, ginger, and cloves.
- Place all of the cake's ingredients in a large bowl and combine well. Just until mixed, whisk the dry and wet ingredients together. Before using, let the dough rest in the refrigerator for an hour.
- Line just two baking sheets and set the oven to 350 degrees. Cover with parchment paper. Put some sugar in a little plate.

- Scoop chilled dough into sugar with a large cookie scoop then coat by rolling place 3 inches apart on the prepared baking sheet. Despite its lack of firmness, the dough will remain highly malleable.

- Bake the pies for 14 to 15 minutes, or until the tops are crinkled and the edges are just beginning to firm.

- After 5 minutes of cooling on the baking sheet, transfer to a cooling rack to finish cooling.

62. Thumbprint Cookies

Preparation Time:

5 mins

Total Time:

40 mins

Servings:

35 servings

Ingredients:

- 1-and-a-half cups all-purpose flour
- 0.5 teaspoons of baking powder
- 1/2 teaspoon of kosher salt
- 1 1/2 sticks of softened 3/4 cup butter
- ½ cup of sugar, granulated
- 1 big egg
- One teaspoon of vanilla extract
- 1/3 cup of various jams for frosting cookies

Directions:

- Prepare two baking trays with parchment paper, and set the oven at 350 degrees Fahrenheit. Salt, baking soda, and flour are combined in a big bowl.
- In a separate dish, mix the butter and sugar for about 3 minutes. The dry ingredients can be added in two batches and beaten until thoroughly blended after the egg and vanilla have been added. The balls are then positioned on the baking sheets using a 1" cookie scoop. Make a half-inch-deep imprint with your thumb in the center of each ball. Put a small amount of jam in the middle.
- Bake the cookies for 13 to 14 minutes, or until they have a golden brown crust. Before serving, allow cooling on baking sheets.

63.   Biscochitos

Preparation Time:

35 mins

Total Time:

50 mins

Servings:

50 to 60 servings

Ingredients:

- 2 tablespoons. plus 1/2 cup of granulated sugar
- 1/4 teaspoon cinnamon powder
- 2 sticks of butter, 1 cup
- Crushed anise seeds, 1 1/2 teaspoons
- 1 big egg
- All-purpose flour, 3 cups
- 1.5 teaspoons of baking powder
- 1/2 teaspoon of kosher salt
- 1/4 cup of brandy

Directions:

- Preheat the oven to 350 degrees before beginning to prepare it. Line a sizable baking sheet with parchment paper. In a small bowl, combine 2 tbsp. sugar and 1 tsp. cinnamon.
- In a larger bowl, combine the remaining sugar, anise seeds, and butter or lard. Using a whisk or hand mixer, beat the mixture for 3 to 4 minutes, or until it is fluffy and light. The egg should be mixed in all the way before being added.
- Salt, baking powder, and flour are all whisked together in a medium bowl. Stir to blend before folding in half of the flour mixture and half of the brandy. Once more combine brandy with all of the dry ingredients.
- Spread the dough out to a thickness of 14 inches on a clean, lightly dusted surface. Preferable shapes should be cut out and placed on a prepared baking sheet.
- Bake the cookies in the oven for 10 to 14 minutes, or until the bottoms are lightly browned.

64.   Sugar Cookie Trees

Preparation Time:

20 mins

Total Time:

30 mins

Servings:

8 servings

Ingredients:

- One tube of sugar cookie batter
- 1/2 cup softened butter
- 2 cups of powdered sugar
- 1 teaspoon of vanilla essence
- 2 tablespoons of heavy cream
- Food dyes in green
- 1/2 teaspoon salt
- Nonpareils for Christmas
- Yellow Mini-M&Ms; Sprinkle Stars

Directions:

- A medium cookie sheet with parchment paper should be preheated to 350 degrees. Make balls ranging in size from 1 to 3 teaspoons. The cookies should be baked for five minutes on a baking sheet; then, the smallest ones should be removed and baked for three to four more minutes. Remove from the oven, and let cool on a cooling rack.
- In a big bowl, beat the butter with a hand mixer until it is light and fluffy. Then add the salt, food colorings, vanilla, heavy cream, and powdered sugar, and whisk everything together until it is thoroughly incorporated. Continue adding food colorings until the desired tint is achieved.
- Transfer to a piping bag fitted with a medium star tip, and then pipe the batter onto the cake.
- Apply frosting in a circle to the enormous cookie. The second-largest cookie should be placed on top, followed by the frosting-filled circle of the final cookie. On the tiniest cookie, pipe a small dot. Sprinkles and a sprinkled star or a small yellow m&m can be added to the top of the cake. Serve.

65.   Chocolate Hazelnut Thumbprint Cookies

Preparation Time:

1 hrs 30 mins

Total Time:

1 hrs 45 mins

Servings:

4 dozens

Ingredients:

- 1 1/2 cups of all-purpose flour; 3/4 cup of raw hazelnuts; and 1/2 cup of unsweetened cocoa powder.

  - 0.5 teaspoons baking soda
- 3/4 teaspoon of kosher salt
- divided between 8 tablespoons of unsalted butter
- 4 ounces of semisweet chocolate chips
- 2/3 cup split granulated sugar
- 1/2 cup packed brown sugar
- 1 large egg
- 1 teaspoon pure vanilla essence
- 1 tablespoon whole milk
- 1/2 cup Nutella

Directions:

- Preheat the oven to 350oF. Hazelnuts should be roasted for 10 to 12 minutes on a rimmed baking sheet, or until fragrant and deeper in color. Allow for a brief period of cooling. Hazelnuts can be ground into fine powder in a food processor.
- In the meantime, make a thick paste in a medium basin by mixing flour, cocoa powder, baking soda, and salt. Hazelnuts ground should be added to the mixture.
- Melt the chocolate and 4 tablespoons of butter in a bowl that can be placed in the microwave. Cook for about a minute, swirl after each burst in 15-second increments in the microwave. Allow cooling for a few minutes before using.
- Beat brown sugar, 13 cups granulated sugar, and the remaining butter Using a hand mixer or a stand mixer with a paddle attachment, beat the ingredients in a sizable basin for two minutes. Beat for a minute after adding the egg, vanilla, and milk to the bowl. After adding the melted chocolate mixture, Beat the mixture consistently until it is well-combined. Flour should be added to a low-speed mixer and blended completely.

- Using parchment paper, cover two large baking sheets. Pour 1 cup of granulated sugar onto the plate and evenly distribute. Working your way through the dough, place mounds of it one at a time onto the baking sheets. They should then be formed into balls, dusted with sugar, and positioned 2 inches apart on prepared baking pans. Using your thumbs, gently press into each of the balls.
- The oven's upper and lower shelves should be preheated to 350 degrees. Seven to eight minutes, flipping the baking sheets once halfway through. Rein dent the cookie's indentation when it comes out of the oven with a daring thumb.

- It should be slightly runny but not utterly liquid after about 20 seconds of microwave cooking. Indent each cookie with a half-teaspoon of Nutella while they're still warm.

66.   Oatmeal Cranberry White Chocolate Cookies

Preparation Time:

15 mins

Total Time:

1 hrs 20 mins

Servings:

5 dozens

Ingredients:

- 1 cup (2 sticks) room temperature butter
  - 3/4 cup granulated sugar
  - 3/4 cup brown sugar
  - 2 large eggs
  - 1 teaspoon of pure vanilla extract
  - 1 1/2 cups of all-purpose flour
  - 1/2 teaspoon of kosher salt
  - 1 teaspoon of baking soda
  - 2 teaspoons of ground cinnamon
  - 3 cups of old-fashioned rolled oats
  - 1 cup of sweetened dried cranberries
  - 1 cup of white chocolate chips are all needed to make this recipe

Directions:

- Set the oven rack in the middle and preheat the oven to 350 °F to begin preparing it. Two baking sheets have parchment paper on them; place them aside.
- Using a stand mixer or a large bowl with a hand mixer, cream the butter and sugars together on medium speed until frothy and light. Add each egg one at a time, fully incorporating it before adding the next, then add the vanilla until the consistency is just right.
- In a big bowl, combine the flour, salt, baking soda, and cinnamon.
- You should incorporate the dry ingredients and oats into the creamed butter mixture. Cranberries and white chocolate chips can be added now.
- Place 2 tablespoon-sized Place the cookies on the baking sheets 2 inches apart. (For this, a medium-sized cookie scoop works well.)
- Bake the corners for 10 to 12 minutes, or until golden brown. The cookies should be placed on a rack to complete cooling.

67.   Crème Brulee Sugar Cookies

Preparation Time:

10 mins

Total Time:

50 mins

Servings:

40 servings

Ingredients:

<u>**FOR THE COOKIES**</u>
1 large egg
1 tbsp. pure vanilla extract
3/4 cup (1 1/2 sticks) softened butter
1/2 cup packed brown sugar
1/2 cup granulated sugar
2 cups all-purpose flour
2 tablespoons cornstarch
1 tablespoon baking soda
1/4 teaspoon kosher salt
<u>**FOR THE FROSTING**</u>
• One (8-ounce) block of softened cream cheese
- 1/4 cup of granulated sugar
- 1 1/4 cups of powdered sugar
- 1 teaspoon of pure vanilla extract

Directions:

- On two baking pans that have been lined with paper, bake at 350 degrees for at least 10 minutes. The butter and sugars are creamed for 3 to 4 minutes. Stir well after adding the egg and vanilla essence.
- Before incorporating it into the wet components, the flour, baking soda, and salt should first be whisked together in a separate bowl. It will be a thick dough.
- Using a tiny cookie scoop, place dough balls the size of a tablespoon on cookie trays prepared with parchment. To make the cookies a little flatter, lightly press down on them. The edges should start to brown after 9 to 10 minutes of baking.
- Remove from the oven, let cool for 2 to 3 minutes, then place on a cooling rack.

<u>Make the icing by:</u>

- Once smooth, beat the cream cheese. Once you've added the powdered sugar and vanilla, stir it all together until it's completely smooth.

- In a small bowl, combine the sugar and mix to combine. On the top of each cookie, spread about a tablespoon of frosting and press into granulated sugar to coat the frosting.
- Before serving, caramelize the sugar a kitchen torch, then place it aside to cool. Refrigerate cookies for up to four days.

68.   Snickerdoodle Cookies

Preparation Time:

5 mins

Total Time:

1 hrs

Servings:

33 servings

Ingredients:

• 2 1/2 cups all-purpose flour
• 2 tablespoons cream of tartar
• 1 tablespoon baking soda
• 1 tablespoon kosher salt
• 1 cup softened butter
• 1 1/4 cups divided granulated sugar
• 1/2 cup packed brown sugar
• 2 large eggs
• 1 tablespoon ground cinnamon

Directions:

- Simply warm your oven to 350 degrees Fahrenheit to get started. Put two large baking sheets together in a row using parchment paper. Completely combine in a medium basin. baking soda, salt, and flour. Butter and 1 cup granulated sugar and brown sugar should be beaten until light and fluffy making use of a hand mixer in a different bowl.
- Add the eggs and beat until combined. Utilizing a spatula, incorporate the wet and dry ingredients.
- Combine the remaining 14 cups of cinnamon and sugar in a small basin.
- Using a medium cookie scoop, form the dough into balls that are about 1 1/2 inches in diameter. Next, coat the balls with cinnamon sugar by rolling them in it. About 2 people should be seated "on preheated baking trays.
- Bake the cookies now for 12 minutes, or until they begin to crack. After the cookies have cooled on the trays for five minutes, move them to a wire rack to finish cooling.

69. Peppermint Pattie Stuffed Chocolate Cookies

Preparation Time:

10 mins

Total Time:

20 mins

Servings:

14 servings

Ingredients:

- 1 box of cake mix, chocolate
- 1 teaspoon baking soda
  - 2 large eggs
  - 1/2 cup canola oil
  - 14 York Peppermint Pattie Minis
  - decorative sprinkles

Directions:

- Line baking pans in the most efficient manner with parchment paper and preheat the oven to 350°. The cake mix and baking powder should be combined in a large bowl, and the eggs and oil should be combined in a another bowl. The dry ingredients should be blended thoroughly with the wet ingredients in a separate basin.
- Shape dough into miniature balls your hands, please. Roll out the dough to completely encase a Peppermint Patty, then form a flattened ball. On a baking sheet, repeat with the remaining dough.
- The top should be golden brown after baking for 8 to 10 minutes. After a brief period of cooling on the baking sheet, transfer to a wire rack to finish cooling.

70.   Pignoli Cookies

Preparation Time:

10 mins

Total Time:

45 mins

Servings:

16 servings

Ingredients:

crumbled 12 oz of almond paste
Sugar, powdered, 1 1/3 cups
2 substantial egg whites
Kosher salt, 3/4 teaspoon
Pine nuts, one cup

Directions:

- Effective style baking sheets with parchment paper and Set the oven to 350 degrees.
- Place all of the ingredients in a food processor and pulse several times to thoroughly blend them. Put the pine nuts on a plate that isn't too deep.
- Form 1 piece of dough by kneading it with slightly dampened hands "a pair of 1" balls. Sprinkle pine nuts over balls and lightly press to adhere. Roll them into 1-1/2-inch balls, then arrange them on the prepared sheets a full 360 degrees around.
- Bake the dish now for 16 to 18 minutes, or until the top is brown.
- Transfer the cookies to a wire rack to complete cooling once they have cooled on the baking sheet for one minute.

71.Icebox Cookies

Preparation Time:

20 mins

Total Time:

1 hrs 50 mins

Servings:

25 servings

Ingredients:

<u>**FOR THE COOKIE**</u>
- All-purpose Flour
- Baking Powder
- Kosher Salt
- 1 cup (2 sticks) butter are all required.
- 1 large egg
- 1/2 cup granulated sugar
- 1/2 cup packed brown sugar
- 1 teaspoon pure vanilla extract

<u>**OPTIONAL MIX-INS**</u>
- 1/2 cup dried fruit
- 1/2 cup toasted coconut
- 1/2 cup chopped candy canes
- 1/4 cup cocoa powder
- 1 cup chopped nuts, such as almonds, pecans, or pistachios;
- 1 cup chopped chocolate (5 oz)
- 1 cup chopped toffee
- 1 cup chopped pretzels
- 2 tablespoons of sprinkles
- 1 teaspoon of instant espresso
- 1 teaspoon of spices, like ground cinnamon

Directions:

- While whisking, combine the flour, baking soda, and salt in a medium bowl. Using a hand mixer, combine the butter and sugar in a big basin (or a stand mixer with a paddle attachment). Add the vanilla after beating in the egg, then beat again to ensure a smooth mixture.
- Work harder than necessary until the dry ingredients are barely combined. Beat in any desired mix-ins until they are incorporated.
- On a piece of plastic wrap, roll the dough into a log that is 2 inches thick. To get it to the proper temperature, place in the refrigerator for at least an hour.

125

- 350 degrees Fahrenheit should be the oven's setting. Two sizable baking sheets should be covered in parchment paper. Cut cookies about 12" thick with a sharp knife, then arrange them on the pans.
- At this point, the edges should have browned, and the center should be firm about 14 minutes.

72.   Cowboy Cookies

Preparation Time:

15 mins

Total Time:

50 mins

Servings:

3 dozens

Ingredients:

- Two sticks of softened butter
- one cup of granulated sugar
- one cup of packed brown sugar
- one tablespoon of pure vanilla extract
- two large eggs
- two cups of all-purpose flour
- two tablespoons of baking soda
- one tablespoon of ground cinnamon
- one tablespoon of kosher salt
- one cup of semisweet chocolate chips are the ingredients

• One cup of peanut butter chips.

- Old-fashioned rolled oats, unsweetened coconut flakes, and chopped pecans total 2 cups (8 oz.)

Directions:

- Just two large baking sheets should be lined with parchment paper, and the oven should be preheated to 375 degrees.
- A hand mixer should be used to beat butter and sugars in a big bowl for about two minutes, or until they are light and fluffy. Add eggs and vanilla extract gradually to the batter, mixing well after each addition.
- Separately combine the flour, baking soda, baking powder, cinnamon, and salt. Now combine the butter and flour, and thoroughly combine. Chocolate, peanut butter and pecans can be added at this point.
- Distribute 1 1/2-inch dough balls on the baking sheets at a distance of about 2 inches.
- Bake the cookies for 10 to 12 minutes, lightly browning them.

73.　Pumpkin Chocolate Cookies

Preparation Time:

15 mins

Total Time:

1 hrs

Servings:

35 servings

Ingredients:

- 2 14 cup universal Flour
- Baking soda, 1 teaspoon
- Pumpkin pie spice, 1 teaspoon
- Kosher salt, 1/2 teaspoon
- 1 c. (2 sticks) melted unsalted butter
- 3/4 cup of brown sugar in bags
- Granulated sugar, half a cup
- Pumpkin purée, 3/4 cup
- One big egg
- Pure vanilla extract, 2 teaspoons
- Semisweet chocolate chips in two cups

Directions:

- Line two sizable baking sheets with parchment paper and heat the oven to 375 degrees.
- In a small basin, combine the flour, baking soda, pumpkin spice, and salt.
- In a big bowl, combine the butter and sugars and beat them with a hand mixer until they are light and fluffy. Well combine the flour, baking powder, sugar, and salt. Add chocolate chips after beating on low speed until no raw flour is visible. Put the dough in the fridge for 30 minutes.
- On the baking sheets, make 1" balls and space them 2 inches apart. Bake for about 12 minutes, or until the edges are puffy and brown.

74.   Red Velvet Crinkle Cookies

Preparation Time:

10 mins

Total Time:

35 mins

Servings:

2 dozens

Ingredients:

- All-purpose flour 2 cups
- unsweetened cocoa powder 2 tablespoons
- Baking powder: 1 1/4 tsp
- baking soda: 1/4 tsp
- Kosher salt 1/2 tsp
- 1/2 cup (1 stick) baking utensils
- Two large eggs
- two teaspoons of pure vanilla essence
- one tablespoon of red food coloring
- 3/4 cup of granulated sugar are required

Directions:

- Start by just preheating Before starting, preheat the oven at 325 degrees and prepare two baking trays with parchment paper. In a larger bowl, whisk together the flour, cocoa powder, baking powder, baking soda, and salt.
- Using a hand mixer, beat sugar and baking sticks until frothy in a separate large dish. Add vanilla and red food colouring, beating in between each addition of egg. Just enough to blend the dry ingredients is required.
- Form a ball out of approximately 1 tablespoon of dough, then coat it with powdered sugar coat it thoroughly. Reroll each ball in powdered sugar and continue the process with the remaining dough.
- Simply bake the cookies for 10 to 12 minutes right now or till the time they've flat and set in the middle, on a baking sheet preheated with nonstick spray.
- After that, move to a wire rack and allow to fully cool.

75.   3 ingredient Sugar Cookies

Preparation Time:

10 mins

Total Time:

30 mins

Servings:

12 servings

Ingredients:

• one stick and two tablespoons softened salted butter
Sprinkles
- one cup all-purpose flour
- 1/3cup granulated sugar (optional)

Directions:

- Pre-heat the oven to 325 °F. While completely mixing both butter and sugar in a large bowl with a hand mixer, add the flour. After shaping into 1" balls, the cookies should be spaced roughly 2 inches apart on a baking pan. Cookies can be made into discs and then topped with sprinkles.
- Cook the biscuits for 15 to 17 mins, or till they begin to turn brown around the edges.

76.   Christmas Light Cookies

Preparation Time:

10 mins

Total Time:

2 hrs 30 mins

Servings:

two dozens

Ingredients:

FOR THE COOKIES
- All-purpose Flour
- Baking Powder
- Kosher Salt 2 cups of it are required (1 stick) Baking sticks from the country crock
- One large egg
- one cup granulated sugar
- one teaspoon pure vanilla extract

FOR THE ICING
- Black decorating gel
- two cups of powdered sugar
- two tablespoons of light corn syrup
- two tablespoons plus 1 tablespoon of milk
- 1/2 cup of mini M&Ms.

Directions:

- Inside a medium basin, simultaneously whisk flour, baking soda, and salt. Inside a large basin, whisk sugar and Country Crock Baking Sticks with a hand blender until foamy. After pounding, add the vanilla and egg. The dry ingredients are then added, and they are very briefly mixed. Put plastic wrap on the disc, then shape it into a disc. Refrigerate for one hour to chill.
- 2 baking sheets should be lined Using parchment Stretch out all the dough to a width of 1/4 inch "hefty" on the a board dusted with flour. Remove 3 from the mix. "Place rounds on baking sheets that have been preheated. Thirty minutes should be put in the freezer.
- Bake for 16 to 18 minutes, or until the edges are just beginning to turn golden. Permit cooling to finish.
- In a medium bowl, thoroughly combine milk, corn syrup, and powdered sugar. Thin with a few drops of milk if necessary.
- To create an even circle, smooth the icing using the back of a spoon on each cookie before topping with an additional 1 tablespoon of icing.
- Create two thin lines across the cookie with black decorating gel to resemble a string of lights. As a source of illumination, place M&Ms along the black line. Let the timer run out.

77. Leg Lamp Cookies

Preparation Time:

5 mins

Total Time:

50 mins

Servings:

3 dozen

Ingredients:

- 1/4 cup of all-purpose flour

- 1 (16.5 oz.) log of refrigerated sugar cookie dough Flour

- 3 (0.67-oz.) tubes of black gel icing
- 18 Reese's Big Cups
- 1/4 c. yellow decorating icing
- 3 tbsp. peanut butter

Directions:

- Turn the oven's dial to 350 degrees Fahrenheit. In a big bowl, mix the flour and cookie dough. Draw heeled-leg shapes with a paring knife on 1/8-inch-thick cookie dough. The cookies should be baked for around 10 minutes, or until the edges are just starting to turn golden brown. After placing on a cooling rack, let the food cool fully.
- Using cookie icing, draw a heel and crosshatch pattern on the leg lamp to resemble fishnet stockings. About 10 minutes in the fridge will do the trick.
- Using a serrated knife, slice each of Reese's cups in half lengthwise. Place one Reeses cup on the top of each sugar cookie with a small dollop of peanut butter on the cut side.
- In a small dish, combine the yellow icing with 2 teaspoons of water. Using a tiny silicone spatula or pastry brush, pipe icing into the nooks and crannies of the peanut butter cup to mimic a yellow lampshade. Refrigerate for 10 minutes to allow the mixture to harden.

78.   Meringue Cookies

Preparation Time:

5 mins

Total Time:

4 hrs 20 mins

Servings:

3 dozen

Ingredients:

• 4 egg whites
  - 1/3 cup granulated sugar
  - 2/3 cup powdered sugar
  - 1/2 teaspoon of pure vanilla essence
  - 1/8 teaspoon of cream of tartar
  - 1/8 teaspoon of kosher salt

Directions:

- Simply preheat the oven to 225 degrees Fahrenheit to begin preparing it. To blend sugars, all you need is a small bowl. Whip the egg whites with an electric mixer until they reach firm peaks. After beating until frothy, add salt and cream of tartar. Add vanilla to the mixture to incorporate it.
- A tablespoon at a time, while swirling continually, add the sugar. Egg whites should be glossy and stiff.
- To pipe the mixture onto a cake, use a piping bag and a large star tip. Use parchment paper to line two baking sheets. Meringues are piped onto a baking sheet.
- After baking for one hour, After turning off the oven, keep the meringues closed for three to eight hours.

79. Cake Mix Christmas Cookies

Preparation Time:

15 mins

Total Time:

25 mins

Servings:

12 servings

Ingredients:

- 1 box of cake mix, vanilla
- 1 teaspoon baking soda
- 2 large eggs and half a cup of canola oil.
- 1/2 c. red and green sprinkles

Directions:

- The oven should be preheated to 350 degrees, and two baking sheets should be lined with parchment paper. The cake mix and baking powder should be combined in a large bowl, and the eggs and oil should be combined in a another bowl. The dry ingredients should be blended thoroughly with the wet ingredients in a separate basin. Stir in the sprinkles until they are evenly distributed. Make little dough balls with your hands, then put them on the baking sheets.
- Prepare by baking for seven to nine minutes. After a brief period of cooling on the baking sheet, move to a wire rack to finish cooling.

80. Meringue Wreath Cookies

Preparation Time:

25 mins

Total Time:

40 mins

Servings:

2 to 3 servings

Ingredients:

- Two big, room-temperature egg whites
- 1/4 teaspoon cream of tartar
- 1/2 cup sugar
- a pinch of kosher salt, 1/2 teaspoon almond essence
- six drops of green food colouring
- one tablespoon of silver sanding sugar
- 4 Pull 'n Peel Twizzlers
- 1/4 cup melted red candy melts

Directions:

- Preheat your oven to 300 degrees. Make a template for the wreaths by drawing circles on parchment paper. A cookie sheet should be lined with parchment, with the pen lines facing down. In a larger bowl, combine the cream of tartar, salt, and sugar.
- Whip egg whites and almond extract using a hand mixer in a sizable basin or the whisk attachment of a stand mixer in the bowl until the mixture begins to foam.
- With the mixer running at high speed, gradually add the sugar mixture as stiff peaks start to form. Whip in the green food dye until well-combined.
- Using your drawn guides, fill a piping bag with meringue and pipe onto a cookie sheet. Toss in a few extra flourishes.
- Until almost stiff to the touch, bake for 13 to 15 minutes. Wait for 2 to 3 minutes before removing it from the oven, after which time it should be firm enough to be removed from the oven. Allow for complete cooling.
- String Twizzlers together to make the bow decoration. Trim each string to 3 inches and form it into a bow. Put them together with melted candy melts. Wait for the candy to harden before attempting to eat it.
- Let the remaining candy melts harden before attaching the bows to the wreaths.

81.Nutella Stuffed Cookies

Preparation Time:

15 mins

Total Time:

1 hrs 25 mins

Servings:

24 servings

Ingredients:

• 2 cups of all-purpose flour
• 1 1/2 cups of Nutella
• 1 cup of softened butter (2 sticks)
  • 1 cup of packed brown sugar
  • 1/2 cup of sugar, 2 large eggs
  • 2 tablespoons of milk
  • 2 teaspoons of pure vanilla extract
  • 1 cup of unsweetened dark cocoa powder
  • 1 teaspoon of baking soda
  • 1 teaspoon of kosher salt
  • 1 teaspoon of flaky sea salt

Directions:

• Use parchment paper to cover a baking sheet. 1-tablespoon balls of Nutella should be spooned onto the baking sheet and baked as directed.
• Using a hand mixer, beat the butter and sugars in a sizable basin until they are light and fluffy. Add the flour and cocoa powder after blending the egg yolks, milk, and vanilla extract. While the Nutella is in the freezer, chill the dough.
• Line a baking sheet with parchment paper to prepare it and preheating the oven to 350 degrees.
• Cookie dough should be scooped into a pancake-like circle and flattened. If more dough is required to completely encase the Nutella ball, add it and pinch the corners together to seal. On a prepared baking sheet, repeat the process with the remaining dough and the frozen Nutella spacing cookies 2 inches apart.
• The cookies should be baked for 15 minutes, or until they puff up. Before serving, allow the pan to cool for 5 minutes.

82.   Rolo Ornament Cookies

Preparation Time:

5 mins

Total Time:

1 hrs

Servings:

16 servings

Ingredients:

- 1 (16.5-oz.) log sugar cookie dough
- 1 can of vanilla frosting
- Mini M&Msdecorative sprinkles
- 16 Rolos

Directions:

- A parchment-lined baking sheet is essential for this recipe. Cookie dough can be scooped into tablespoon-sized rounds and rolled into balls.
- Bake the cookies for 10 to 15 minutes, or until they are just starting to turn brown around the edges. Allow them cool a little on the baking sheets, then move to a wire rack to finish cooling.
- Decorate the cookies with M&Ms and sprinkles after they've cooled. Toss in a Rolo.

83.   Milano Reindeer Cookies

Preparation Time:

20 mins

Total Time:

12 hrs

Servings:

15 servings

Ingredients:

- 15 pretzels
- 1/4 cup marshmallow fluff
- 15 Milano cookies
- 1 teaspoon powdered sugar
- 1 can vanilla frosting from the shop
- 30 brown tiny M&Ms
- 15 red M&Ms are the ingredients (full size)

Directions:

- The centre of a pretzel can be cut in two horizontally. Press each half of a pretzel into the top of a Milano cookie after dipping the edges in Marshmallow Fluff. So that the Fluff doesn't stick, sprinkle some powdered sugar on top of it.
- Turn the Milano cookies over on a baking sheet or tray that has been lined with parchment.
- On each cookie, draw three circles: two for the eyes, one for the nose at the bottom. a No. 3 piping tip in the middle of one of the frosting bags. Pressing a little M&M into the melted white chocolate circles creates the reindeer's eyes.
- Place a red M&M, "M" side down, on the final dollop of frosting and top each biscuit with it.

84.   Cookies 'n Cream Blossom Cookies

Preparation Time:

15 mins

Total Time:

25 mins

Servings:

36 servings

Ingredients:

- 3/4 cup softened butter
- 1 cup sugar; 1 large egg
- 1 teaspoon pure vanilla extract
- 1 1/4 cups all-purpose flour
- 1/2 cup dark cocoa powder
- 1 teaspoon baking soda
- 2 teaspoons cornstarch
- 36 unwrapped Cookies 'n' Crème

Directions:

- Cook at 350 degrees for at least ten minutes before you begin. In a large bowl, beat the butter and sugar with a hand mixer for three to four minutes, or until fluffy.
- Before serving, fully combine the ingredients with the egg and vanilla.
- To prepare the batter, combine the wet and dry ingredients in a different bowl.
- Place tablespoons of cookie dough, rolled into balls, on an already heated cookie sheet.
- Bake in the oven for 6 to 8 minutes, or until the centers are mostly set and the rims are golden brown. After taking them out of the oven, immediately press a Hershey's Kiss into the center of each.
- Before moving the cookies to a cooling rack to finish cooling, give them two to three minutes to cool. Cookies can be stored at room temperature in an airtight container for up to three days.

85.   Melted Snowman Cookies

Preparation Time:

20 mins

Total Time:

45 mins

Servings:

12 servings

Ingredients:

- Six marshmallows
- halved at an angle, together with a dozen baked sugar cookies
- Black cookie icing or melted chocolate for decorating
- White cookie icing for decorating
- 24 little M&Ms for buttons
- 24 chocolate jimmies for arms
- 12 orange jimmies for noses

Directions:

- Make melted blobs of white cookie icing by spreading it on sugar cookies.
- Make eyes and a smile out of black cookie icing on some marshmallows! (or smirk).
- To give the marshmallow a nose, stick an orange jimmy in it.
- Make a neck for the marshmallow by wrapping it in cookie icing and adding more.
- To decorate, place chocolate jimmies for the arms and M&Ms for the buttons on cookie icing.

86.   Sugar Cookie Bites

Preparation Time:

15 mins

Total Time:

1 hrs

Servings:

36 servings

Ingredients:

- 1 1/4 cups of all-purpose flour
- 3 tablespoons of powdered sugar
- 1/4 teaspoon of kosher salt
- 1/2 cup of unsalted butter.
- Vanilla buttercream
- Food dyes in red and green
- red and green sprinkles

Directions:

- Set the oven temperature to 325 °F. Butter, flour, sugar, and salt should all be added to a food processor and processed until completely smooth. Using your hands, The dough should be worked in a sizable bowl until it comes together.
- Make the dough into a 12"-thick square on waxed paper. Make 1/2-inch squares out of the dough. On a sizable baking sheet, spread the dough, and bake at 350 degrees for 20 minutes. Depending on the thickness of the cookies, the baking time should be 18 to 20 minutes. Allow for complete cooling.
- Make three small bowls of vanilla frosting. Make one bowl red and the other green using red food coloring. Make frosted cookies festive by decorating them with red and green sprinkles.

87. Pecan Pie Thumbprint Cookies

Preparation Time:

30 mins

Total Time:

1 hrs

Servings:

24 servings

Ingredients:

FOR COOKIES:
- All-purpose flour (1 3/4 cups)
- baking powder (1/2 teaspoon)
- kosher salt, 1/2 tsp
- melted butter, 3/4 cup (1 1/2 sticks)
- 1 large egg
- 1/2 cup granulated sugar
- 1 teaspoon pure vanilla extract

FOR FILLING:
- 1 stick of butter
- 1/2 cup of granulated sugar
- 1/4 cup of dark corn syrup
- 1/2 teaspoon of kosher salt
- 2/3 cup of pecans that have been finely chopped
- For drizzling, caramel

Directions:

For cookies:

- Combine all the ingredients, including the salt, baking soda, and flour, in a small bowl. Using an electric mixer, beat the butter and sugar in a big bowl until they are light and fluffy. Egg and vanilla should be beaten first, followed by the flour mixture. Set the temperature of the oven to 350 degrees Fahrenheit.
- Make 1" balls out of the dough by rolling it out. Before baking, form a little dimple with your thumb in the center of each ball.
- Bake the cookies for 13 to 14 minutes, or until the edges are lightly browned.

Fill in the gaps:

- In a small saucepan, combine the butter, corn syrup, sugar, and salt. Heat until boiling. After boiling for 2 minutes over medium heat, it should thicken. Add the pecans after that. Before adding the filling, let the cookies cool.
- Before serving, add a drizzle of caramel.

88. Mint Chocolate Chip Cookies

Preparation Time:

15 mins

Total Time:

45 mins

Servings:

20 servings

Ingredients:

- 2 cups of all-purpose flour
- 1 cup of softened butter
- 1 cup of granulated sugar
- plus, additional for dusting
- 1 big egg
- 1 teaspoon of peppermint essence
- 6 drops of green food coloring
- 1/2 teaspoon each of baking soda
- baking powder, and salt
- 1 cup of chopped Andes mints

Directions:

- A parchment-lined baking sheet is essential for this recipe. The butter and sugar are combined in a big basin and mixed with a hand mixer until the mixture is light and fluffy. Then, until everything is well-combined, add the egg and peppermint extract.
- Mix the dry ingredients thoroughly with a wooden spoon or a mixer with a paddle attachment. If desired, color the dough green. Add chopped Andes to the mixture.
- Form small balls with a small scoop and set them about 2" apart on baking pans, according to the recipe. Add some sugar to the top.
- Bake the cookies for 10 to 12 minutes, or until they have swelled and hardened.
- Then, transfer to a wire rack and allow to cool for an additional 10 minutes.

89. Budy the Elf Cookies

Preparation Time:

5 mins

Total Time:

30 mins

Servings:

10 servings

Ingredients:

- One bag of 12-ounce white chocolate chips
- 3 c. crispy chow mein noodles
- 1/2 c. marshmallow bits
- chocolate syrup
- rainbow sprinkles

Directions:

- Microwave white chocolate at 30 second intervals, stirring in between (about 2 minutes).Chow Mein noodles and marshmallows should be added to a large bowl.
- Drop spoonsful of the batter onto a baking sheet covered with parchment paper. Put it in the fridge until set, about 15 minutes, then top with a sprinkle of fudge sauce and rainbow sprinkles.

90. Caramel Gingerbread Cookies Bars

Preparation Time:

15 mins

Total Time:

1 hrs 15 mins

Servings:

9 to 12 servings

Ingredients:

FOR THE COOKIE BARS
- 3/4 cup softened unsalted butter
- 1 cup gently packed brown sugar
- 1 big egg
- 3 tablespoons molasses
- 2 1/4 cups all-purpose flour
- 2 1/2 teaspoons ground ginger
- 1 teaspoon cinnamon
- 1/4 teaspoon nutmeg; pinch of cloves
- 1 teaspoon baking soda
- 1/4 teaspoon kosher salt

FOR THE FROSTING
• 1/2 cup of room temperature unsalted butter
Sprinkles
- 2 cups powdered sugar
- 5 tablespoons caramel

Directions:

- Cover the bottom and sides of a 9" × 9" Bake at 350 ° after covering the baking sheet with foil.
- Earlier continuing, make sure the butter and sugar are thoroughly blended. The egg and molasses should be thoroughly combined before being added.
- Before adding the flour to the wet ingredients, combine mixture in a different bowl along with the salt, bicarbonate soda, and bicarbonate of soda, and kneading until a homogeneous dough is produced. For 30 minutes, put the dough in the fridge.

- Cook this dough for between 18 and 20 mins, or until crisp & golden. When removing the pan from the oven, let it rest. Terminate the bars from the pan when they are completely cooled.

Making the icing:

- Using an electric mixer, whip the butter into a smooth paste. Once the powdered sugar and caramel have been thoroughly combined, when smooth, add more powdered sugar and stir.
- Top the bars with frosting, then devour. Serve in third-cut squares. Keep in an airtight container for up to 4 days.

91.Sprinkle Cookies

Preparation Time:

five mins

Total Time:

30 mins

Servings:

23servings

Ingredients:

• one box of Funfetti cake batter
• one teaspoon baking soda
- Two large eggs
- One stick of softened butter
- One teaspoon of pure vanilla extract
- 1/2cup of rainbow sprinkles

Directions:

- Use parchment to line baking sheets and preheat the oven to 350 degrees Fahrenheit.
- Cutting-edge a big basin, combine the cake mix and baking powder. Then, fold the sprinkles after adding the eggs, butter, and vanilla.These cookies should be spaced about it an inch across a baking tray after the dough has been divided in equal portions.
- To achieve a light golden brown colour, For 12 to 13 minutes, bake. Allow it to cool.

92. Candy Canes Cookies

Preparation Time:

45mins

Total Time:

One hrs

Servings:

24 servings

Ingredients:

- two sticks softened salted butter
  - One cup powdered sugar
  - One big room-temperature egg
  - One tsp. vanilla
  - 1 1/2 tsp. peppermint essence
  - Three cups all-purpose flour
  - 1/2 to 1tsp. red food coloring
  - optionally, three crushed candy canes.

Directions:

- Butter and sugar should be softened and placed in a big bowl . Using a hand mixer, beat for 2-3 minutes at medium speed . Add the egg, vanilla, and extract of peppermint. The Flour should be added in one-cup increments, with each addition being thoroughly mixed in before moving on to the next one. Scrape the bowl's bottom and sides as necessary.
- With the remaining portion of the dough, make a 1-inch-thick disc and return it into the basin. A plastic wrap-wrapped dish should be refrigerated for one hour.

- Stir the red food coloring thoroughly with the leftover batter in the pan.Stir slowly on low until all the colourings have been incorporated (Add more food colouring until the appropriate shade of red is achieved.)Make a 1-inch-thick disc out of the red dough by scraping it out of the bowl and kneading Several times on a spotless surface. Take out and discard the plastic wrap after an hour of cooling.

- Use parchment paper to line two large baking sheets. Turn the oven on to 375ºF.
- After the dough has been unwrapped, pinch out 1/2-tablespoon portions of each color. Stretch every rubber round into a 5-inch rope by using you hand and a spotless board.Place the ropes next to each other and twist them together, pinching the tops and bottoms of each rope to hold them in place. Form

into a candy cane shape on the sheet trays with care. Continually form the cookies by rolling, twisting, and twisting.

- Bake the cookies for 12 min, or until the tops of the white dough start to turn brown. If desired, immediately after they are removed from the oven, decorate with crushed candy canes. The baked items should cool completely on the cooking pans before even being transferred to a cooling rack. For up to a week, store between sheets of parchment in an opaque box at room temperature.

93. Spritz Cookies

Preparation Time:

25 mins

Total Time:

1 hrs 40 mins

Servings:

40 to 50 servings

Ingredients:

FOR THE COOKIES:
- one cup softened unsalted butter
- 2/3 cup granulated sugar
- one big egg
- two teaspoons vanilla extract
- 1/2teaspoon kosher salt
- 1/4 teaspoon almond extract
- 2 1/2 cups all-purpose flour

FOR DECORATING:
- 1/2cup melted semisweet chocolate chips
- 1/2 cup melted white chocolate chips
- Sparkling sugar
- Finely shredded coconut
- Christmas sprinkles, such as red, white and green nonpareils

Directions:

For cookies:

- Turn the stove's temperature to 375. Use parchment to line 2 baking trays. Start by mixing the butter and sugar for 2 minutes on moderate speed in a stand mixer with a paddle attachment. Sea salt, vanilla, almond, and other flavours can be added to this. Beat for about a minutes at medium speed to properly integrate. The flour should be beaten with a mixer until it is just barely mixed. For thirty min, the dough needs to be covered and chilled in the fridge.

- To use a cookie, press and previously prepared baking sheets, stamp the cookie dough with the desired decorative shapes. The dough can be stamped after being refrigerated for approximately 15 to 30 minutes.
- Cook the biscuits in the oven for 9 to 12 minutes, flipping the baking pans about halfway through. They ought to be just brown. The cookies should cool for 5 minutes on the cooking sheets. On a wire rack, the cakes must cool for around thirty min.
- **<u>Decorating:</u>**
- Small microwave-safe bowls are ideal for semisweet and white chocolate chips. Stir the mixture every 20 seconds, and cook until smooth and melted on high for 1 to 12 minutes. Sprinkle the cookies with sparkling sugar, shredded coconut, and Christmas sprinkles if desired after drizzling the melted chocolate over them.

94. Chocolate Candy Cane Cookies

Preparation Time:

3 mins

Total Time:

3 hrs 9 mins

Servings:

36 servings

Ingredients:

- 2 sticks of salted, somewhat melted fat
- One cup confectioners' sugar
- One big egg
- Two teaspoons of vanilla
- 2 1/2 cups flour
- 1/2 cup unsweetened cocoa powder
- four oz. weight
- one tsp. salt (4 squares) either white baking chocolate or almond bark
- large handful of red or green peppermints

Directions:

- Add powdered sugar to softened butter and Mix well. Following incorporating the egg and vanilla, dish the batter. Till a dough form, gradually incorporate the dry ingredients.
- Refrigerate for two hours, with plastic wrap covering the dough's surface.
- While you wait, unwrap some candy and put inside a container made of plastic. The mix should be pounded with such a mallet until it resembles coarse sand.
- Turn the oven on to 375degrees.
- Distribute the dough into walnut-sized pieces on a cookie sheet. Gently flatten the balls using a smooth, flat surface. To prevent burning, bake for 7 to 9 minutes. After baking, cookies will maintain their original size and shape. After baking, take the food out and let it cool on a wire rack. Allow them to fully cool before handling.
- Place the crushed candy in a bowl. Using a microwave, melt the almond bark. After the cookies have been allowed to cool, use an almond bark coating to coat half of each cookie. The moment the baked almond bark is removed, sprinkle crushed peppermints over both sides. Cool before serving on parchment paper or another nonstick surface.

95. Gingerbread House Cookies

Preparation Time:

3 hours

Total Time:

3hours 18 mins

Servings:

24 servings

Ingredients:

For the Cookie:
• six cups all-purpose flour
• one teaspoon salt
• 1/2 teaspoon each of ground ginger
ground nutmeg
ground cinnamon, and allspice
• 3/4 cup margarine or melted butter
• 1 1/2 cups firmly packed dark brown sugar
• one cup molasses
• two whole eggs
• one teaspoon each of salt and maple extract

For the royal icing:
•   2 pounds of sifted powdered sugar
•   1/3 cup entire milk; and additional entire milk as needed for thinning
• Two large whole egg whites
• A variety of candies, sprinkles, and other toppings

Directions:

•   Mix salt, cinnamon, ginger, cloves, and allspice in a large mixing bowl. In a sizable bowl, combine salt, cinnamon, ginger, cloves, and allspice. Get rid of.
•   Brown sugar and margarine (or butter) should froth up when mixed in a mixer.The molasses needs to drizzled in and thoroughly mixed in, so scrape the bowl a few times to ensure even distribution. Add the eggs and maple extract and stir. Three batches of the flour mixture should be added each one being added until it is completely incorporated.
•   Be sure to chill the dough for at least two hours, while more time is acceptable.
•   Before bringing the two 350 degrees Fahrenheit, remove the chocolate chip cookies. Using 2 pieces of plastic wrap, spread out each half of the dough until it is just flexible enough just to roll (dividing it in half

just makes it more manageable.) After arranging the forms on a baking sheet lined with parchment or a baking mat, bake the forms.

- Cook the biscuits according to the cookie cutters' recommended baking time. They should be baked through but still a little soft after 12 to 15 minutes. Remove with a spatula once it is cool enough just to touch.
- Add milk and sugar powder. In a mixing dish, beat the egg whites till the form stiff peaks but are still droppable into the mixture.
- Glue the candies to the cookies, then use icing as an accent. If you're going to transport or serve the icing, give it time to set up.

96.   Black and White Cookies

Preparation Time:

15mins

Total Time:

30 mins

Servings:

3 servings

Ingredients:

FOR THE COOKIES:
- 1/4 cup of all-purpose Flour
- 12 teaspoon of baking powder
- 12 teaspoon salt
- 1/3 cup milk
- Vanilla extract, half a teaspoon
- Lemon essence, $1/4$ teaspoon
- Unsalted butter, 6 tablespoons, at room temperature
- 1 large egg and $1/2$ cup sugar

FOR THE GLAZE:
- Confectioners' sugar, 1 1/2 cup
- 4 tablespoons milk, split
- Vanilla extract, 1/4 teaspoon
- Unsweetened cocoa powder, $1/4$ cup

Directions:

- While using the ovens, preheat it to 375 ℃. Using silicon mats or parchment paper to line a sheet pan.
- Create a thick paste by combining the flour, baking soda, and salt in a medium mixing bowl. Get rid of.
- In a measuring cup, mix the milk, vanilla, and lemon extracts. Get rid of.
- To use the paddle attachment on a stand mixer, combine both butter and sugar for about 60 seconds at moderate speed. Scrape the bowl's sides with a spatula before adding the egg.
- Slowly pour in the flour mixture, followed by half of the wet ingredients, the other half of the flour mixture, and then the entire milk mixture. Wait until the prior batch, please.
- Slowly pour inside the flour mix, followed by 1/2 of a wet ingredients, other 1/2 of the flour mixture, and then the entire milk mixture. Before adding the next round, ensure that you give the preceding batch time to thoroughly absorb.
- Use a cookie scoop that can hold three teaspoons of cookie dough to distribute the dough onto pan used for baking. Each box ought to contain roughly 8 cookies. Make absolutely sure they are completely cold before cutting into them after cooking.

- Combine the powdered gelatin' sugar with three drops of milk to make the glazes. When you use a fork to fold in the vanilla, cast aside 1/2 of the glaze. The last 1 tablespoon of milk and the chocolate powder should be mixed.
- Once the cookies have cooled, cover them with a glaze made of equal parts chocolate and vanilla. Enjoy the flavor after the glaze has dried.
- It should be noted that in the absence of a stand mixer, hand mixers may be substituted.

97.   Christmas Cherry Cookies

Preparation Time:

1 hrs 15 mins

Total Time:

1 hrs 35 mins

Servings:

36 servings

Ingredients:

- Two ticks of softened butter
- 1/2 cup sugar
- two whole egg yolks
- one tsp. vanilla extract
- one lemon's zest
- one orange's zest
- one lemon's juice
- two cups all-purpose flour
- twice-sifted candied green and red cherries.

Directions:

- The butter and sugar should be well combined to get a light and airy texture.
- Mix the egg yolks, vanilla, orange, lemon, and lime juices and the peels. Use a slotted spoon to clean the bowl, then stir again.
- Include the sifted flour and combine well. The dough should be chilled a minimum of an hour, or until it turns firm.
- Set your oven to 300 degrees when you're ready to cook the cookies. Halve the cherry candies.
- Slice small pieces of dough and place it on a baking tray that has been lined with baking parchment or a cooking mat. Press a cherry half into each ball with the cut side facing up.
- Remove them from the oven just before they begin to brown, then place them somewhere to cool. Place a dry wire rack there.

98.   Chocolate Gingerbread Cookies

Preparation Time:

60 mins

Total Time:

1 hrs 10 mins

Servings:

5 to 6 servings

Ingredients:

- 115 grammes, or half a cup or One stick, of unsalted butter at room temp.
- 1 tablespoon egg yolk; one teaspoon vanilla essence
- 3/4 cup (about 135 grammes) of brown sugar
- One-fourth cup (60 ml) of molasses or golden syrup
- 40 grammes (1/2 cup) of sifted chocolate chips and 245 grammes (1 and 3/4 cups) of ordinary flour.
- Two teaspoons of baking soda each
- salts, nutmeg, cinnamon, and crushed ginger
- 1/4 teaspoon each of melted chocolate for drizzling.

Directions:

- Using an electric mixer on medium speed, In a big mixing bowl, especially directly the butter and sugar. Add molasses and egg white to the mixture. To make the mixture smooth and creamy, beat it once more.
- The dough will begin to form as soon as the ingredients are sifted into a bowl with a mixer. With your hands, Ensure a seamless, round disc out of the dough. The dough needs to be covered in plastic and refrigerated for at least 30 min.
- Turn the oven on to 350 degrees. Fahrenheit (180 degrees C) or 160 degrees C (320 degrees °F) if using a fan. Use parchment or baking paper to cover two cookie sheets or oven trays in preparation. On a surface that has been lightly dusted with flour, Use a rolling pin to roll out the mixture to a thickness of 1/8 inch. When rolling out all the dough, dusted the rolling pin with flour to avoid sticking.
- Put the cookies on the prepared trays after cutting the desired forms are cut out. For 8 to 10 minutes, bake. Place cooling racks for cookies after removing them from the oven. Pour over melted chocolate for a decadent finish.

99. Christmas Pinwheel Cookies

Preparation Time:

2 hrs 45 mins

Total Time:

3 hrs

Servings:

16 servings

Ingredients:

- Two cups of general-purpose
  - $1/2$ tablespoons room temperature unsalted butter
  - 1/2 teaspoon baking powder
  - 1/4 teaspoon salt
  - 3/4 cup sugar
  - One egg
  - One teaspoon vanilla essence
  - 1/2 to 1 teaspoon liquid red food colouring
  - 1/2 to 1 teaspoon liquid green food colouring

Directions:

- Refrigerate it for around thirty minutes. Get rid of.
- In a large bowl, combine the butter and sugar and beat for 1 to 2 minutes, or until fluffy. Incorporate the egg and vanilla completely, scraping the bowl if required.
- In two separate additions, While adding it to the wet components, combine the flour mixture just enough to combine them. As required, scrape the bowl's sides with a spoon.
- After each piece of dough has been rolled into a been divided into thirds. Measuring the pieces is as simple as eyeballing them or using a scale in the kitchen.
- Add the red food colouring to one more piece of dough in the bowl. Beat until the colour is fully incorporated with your mixer. Your mixer paddle or hand mixer blades should be thoroughly cleaned.
- Replenish the bowl with a single piece of dough and colour it green with the food colouring. Your mixer should be used to incorporate the colour thoroughly. The third piece of dough can be left as is.
- Wrap each piece of dough cover it with plastic and shape it into a square. The dough needs to chilled for at least an hour to become firm.
- The dough squares should be taken out of the fridge. Apply parchment paper or waxed paper to the red dough. The dough should be rolled out into a rectangle that is 10 inches across. Maintain the dough sandwiched between two parchment paper sheets.

- Reroll and reroll the remaining two pieces of dough. For best results, Cookie dough should be kept in the fridge for at least 30 minutes.
- Discard the top layer of parchment from each cookie sheet and take the dough out of the refrigerator. The red dough should be spread out on a counter. The non-parchment sides of the white dough should face each other. Make an effort to align the dough's edges as closely as possible.
- The white dough should be free of parchment paper. Place the green, non-parchment side on top of the white, ensuring the edges are aligned. Do not leave the dough covered in parchment paper. Cut the cookie dough into straight lines on the left and right sides using a pizza cutter.
- With great care, roll the dough into a long shape starting with one straightened edge and finishing with the other. To begin, lift the dough with the parchment paper. When the dough log is complete, close the seam and any breaks in the outer red layer by gently pinching the dough.
- When firm the dough log, put it in the refrigerator for about one hours.
- A 350°F oven is a good starting point. Put parchment paper or a silicon cooking mat on a cookie dish to line it.
- Cut the rubber log into ¼ inch pieces using a sharp knife. Until golden and firm to the touch, the cookies should bake for between 12 and 15 minutes.
- Allow the baked goods to cool completely on the baking sheet after removing them from the oven. Eat it right immediately or wait to eat it by sealing it in a container.

100. Shortbread Christmas Cookies

Preparation Time:

15mins

Total Time:

25 mins

Servings:

36 servings

Ingredients:

For the Shortbread Cookies -
- 2 cups of flour
- 1 cup of softened butter
- 1 teaspoon of vanilla extract
- $3/4$ cup of powdered sugar
- 1/2 cup of cornstarch
- 1/2 teaspoon of salt
- 3 − 4 tablespoons of coloured sprinkles

For the Icing –
- Two cups of powdered sugar
- One teaspoon of vanilla
- two-three tablespoons of water, and green food colouring

Directions:

For the Shortbread Cookies:

- Until smooth, In a mixing dish, combine vanilla and butter.
- After combining the all flour mixture, smooth them out (flour, sugar, cornstarch, and salt).Though crumbly and dry, the dough will keep its shape when baked.
- As soon as the dough is done, Confectioners sugar should be added before transferring it to a large parchment paper sheet. About half an inch of the dough should be pressed into the bottom of a square baking dish.
- Place it in the refrigerator for about thirty min.
- Bring out of the fridge and lift with parchment paper you chilled dough.

- Make triangles out of it. The bottom should be light golden brown after 10 minutes at 325 degrees Fahrenheit in the oven.Allow for complete cooling.

For Icing:

- Begin by combining 2 teaspoons of water and two tablespoons of vanilla in a bowl with the powdered sugar.Mix until a homogeneous mixture is achieved.
- Add more water if needed to thin the frosting so it may be drizzled over cookies.
- When drizzling, use the corner of a zip-top bag and a few drops of green food color in the mix.
- Set the biscuits on a parchment-covered baking sheet paper and cut a small opening in the frosting bag using a set of scissors.Pipe or sprinkle across the triangles in a single direction to imitate trees. Before adding sprinkles, if desired, let the icing sit for a few minutes to dry.

Made in the USA
Columbia, SC
08 November 2022

70628220R00089